The Book of Books

THE OLD TESTAMENT RETOLD

The Book of Books

BY

HENRI DANIEL-ROPS

TRANSLATED BY DONAL O'KELLY

ILLUSTRATED BY FRITZ KREDEL

An
ARKIVE
EDITION
FROM SOPHIA INSTITUTE PRESS®

Sophia Institute Press®
Box 5284, Manchester, NH 03108
1-800-888-9344
www.SophiaInstitute.com

The Book of Books is a translation of *Histoire Sainte de mes Filleuls* by Henri Daniel-Rops (Paris, La Colombe, 1955) originally published in English in 1956 by P. J. Kenedy & Sons, New York.

Nihil Obstat: Joannes J. O'Rourke, S.T.L., L.S.S.,
Censor Deputatus Philadelphia, Pa., February 2, 1956

Imprimatur: ✠ J. F. O'Hara, C.S.C.,
Archbishop of Philadelphia, February 11, 1956

Library of Congress Cataloging-in-Publication Data

Daniel-Rops, Henri, 1901-1965.
[Histoire sainte de mes filleuls. English]
The Book of Books : the Old Testament Retold / by Henri Daniel-Rops ; translated by Donal O'Kelly ; illustrated by Fritz Kredel. — Arkive ed.
p. cm.
ISBN 978-1-933184-48-7 (ppbk : alk. paper) 1. Bible. O.T.—History of Biblical events. I. O'Kelly, Donal. II. Title.

BS1197.D33 2009
221.9'5—dc22

2009009132

09 10 11 12 13 14 10 9 8 7 6 5 4 3 2 1

Contents

The Book of Books

I

A Small Nation with a Great Mission

THERE IS IN THIS WORLD one wonderful book which no one has ever tired of reading. Whether you are a boy or a girl, old or young, rich or poor, you may be sure that when you open it, you will find sentences in it that fit your mood of the moment. It is a book for all the hours of your life. If you are so happy that you want to sing aloud in thanksgiving to God, you will find in it magnificent hymns of joy and gratitude. If, on the other hand, you are downcast and sad, it will whisper words of consolation to you that will soften the bitterness of your tears. Truly, this is a wonderful book!

It might have been kept a secret, hidden from the rest of mankind and kept for their own use by a few privileged people. What a pity it would be if this were so, but fortunately it is not, for millions of copies of it have been printed and it has been translated into every human language. It is read in Africa as it is in America, in France as among the Eskimos. Our fathers and grandfathers and their fathers before them, and so back through the centuries, all have read and studied it.

It is the most famous book in the whole world and not even the most beautiful poetry or the most stirring of stories can compare with it.

When you know the reason, it is not surprising that this book should be so wonderful, for it has been inspired by God Himself. Do you realize what that means? It means that ordinary people like you and me set themselves to write out all these things because deep in their hearts some mysterious force made them do so and guided their pens. Is not this an extraordinary fact?

This book is called the Bible, which means in Greek "the Book of Books," the book that exceeds all others and contains more than all others combined. No doubt you have seen a copy of it. Your parents probably have one and if they do not, they should make haste to buy it. Usually it is a very big volume with red or gilt edges and it is often bound in black-grained leather. The printing is usually in very small type, but in spite of this it has more than a thousand pages. From its very appearance alone one can guess that its contents are important. But in spite of this I would not advise you to bury yourself in it in a corner of the family library. You might not be able to draw the right meaning from it, for it is difficult to understand in places, and you would only be told that it was too advanced for your age. Instead, I will relate everything in it to you and, if you agree, we will turn over the pages together. If you read to the end all that I am going to tell you here, you will know a great deal about the "Book of Books"; more indeed than a lot of grown-up people, and I do not think that you will find your reading tiresome.

Let us then open the Bible at random. Many, many centuries ago there was a small nation whose people were in a very unhappy state. Some time before the period of which we speak, these people had settled in Egypt which, as you know, is the country in North Africa through which flows the River Nile.

At first these people lived happily and in peace and then everything was spoiled for them, for the kings of Egypt, who were called the Pharaos, started to persecute them. They were compelled to do the hardest kind of work, under the burning sun, making bricks and erecting all sorts of buildings, and if they did not work quickly enough, crack! the overseer's whip lashed across their shoulders. Worse still, the Pharaos had decreed that all the little boys of this people should be killed at birth. It was horrible!

But God loved this poor oppressed people and He protected them. One day He summoned one of them, who was called Moses, and said to him, "I command you to free your brethren. Your people have always served Me faithfully, and it is My Will that they leave Egypt and that their unhappiness shall cease."

Moses hesitated long before he undertock this dangerous mission. However, he obeyed in the end and appeared before Pharao. "Let my people go from your kingdom," he told him. "Thus says the Lord God of Israel." The king however found it much more convenient to keep all these workers he did not have to pay, and so he refused. Moses then called on God to help him to force Pharao to yield.

An extraordinary series of happenings now took place. Egypt became the victim of one misfortune after another, all of them, of course, sent by God. The waters of the Nile were turned into blood so that all the fishes died; a plague of frogs descended on the country so that frogs were found everywhere—even in the king's own bed. Then came clouds of flies, as numerous as grains of dust; darkness covered the heavens; cattle sickened and died; and great sores broke out on the flesh of the Egyptian people. Finally, after these and several other misfortunes, there appeared the worst disaster of all: the first-born child of every Egyptian family died, struck down mysteriously by the angels of God.

Pharao understood at last. Terrified, he declared that he would allow Moses and all his people to leave his kingdom. Hastily gathering all their poor belongings, they set off in a long column toward Asia. Hardly had they departed, however, than the cruel ruler repented of his decision to let so many workers go. He changed his mind and set out at the head of his troops in pursuit of the fugitives.

In order to travel eastward from Egypt it was necessary to cross the Red Sea (see map on back endpaper). How was this to be done? The fugitives were halted at the seashore; were they then to be recaptured and led back into slavery? No! Once more Moses called on God for help and lo! as though driven back by a terrific gale, the waters of the Red Sea parted, leaving in the center a wide strip of dry land. Hastily Moses led his people along this miraculous high-

way and, just when the last of his people had reached the farther shore, Pharao appeared with his chariots and horsemen. They impetuously followed in pursuit along the dry sea bed when, with a thunderous roar, the divided waters came together, drowning the king and his army in their immense waves.

Here is just one of the stories we read in the Bible. There are hundreds equally exciting; we will go through many of them together. But no doubt there are two questions that have already sprung to your mind: what was the name of this small nation, and why did God take it under His special protection?

These people whom we saw suffering in bondage on the banks of the Nile and fleeing with Moses were called Hebrews or Israelites, and were later on to be known as Jews. As you know, they have survived ever since, and the Jews of our day are truly the descendants of those whose astonishing history you are going to hear. All of you have met Jews at one time or another, and so it will not be hard for you to picture for yourselves what their ancestors looked like.

Generally speaking, the men and women of the Israelites were of moderate height, with black hair, dark complexions, and fine lustrous eyes. They had three outstanding characteristics: curling hair, a rather long nose, and full red lips. In youth, both boys and girls were often exceptionally graceful. Almost all of them were intelligent, gifted equally in the art of poetry and in business ability. As for their faults—and of course like all men they had faults in plenty—it is not worth while discussing them here, for as we read, these faults will become apparent.

They were part of the Semitic race, just as the English, the French, the Italians and most of the other peoples of Europe belong to the Aryan race. They were closely related to the other peoples of antiquity: the Chaldeans, the Assyrians, and the Phenicians. They were also akin to the Arabs who still exist today. And, like the inhabitants of the Arabian desert in our time, the Hebrews in their early days were nomads, that is, they were constantly on the move, following their herds of beasts from one pasture to another, dwelling in tents and living mainly on milk products. Later, much later, they settled down in a country of their own and became tillers of the soil.

They were not a numerous people. At the commencement of their history which we are about to follow, they consisted merely of a few tribes. Much later, when they were organized into a kingdom and at the height of their power, they numbered at the most eight hundred thousand, less than a tenth of the population of New York City. How did it come about then that a people so small in number should have played such an important part in history? Why should we take so much interest in the doings of a few thousand shepherds and desert wanderers?

The answer is a very simple one: it is because this tiny people produced this wonderful book of which we have been speaking. It was these Hebrews, Israelites, Jews, who in the course of centuries, wrote the hundreds upon hundreds of magnificent pages which make up the Bible. At no period of history has any people in the world expressed in writing so many lofty and noble ideas.

Here also is the answer to the second question we asked ourselves: why did God give such special protection to the people of Israel? He did so because this small people was the first of all nations to recognize and worship the True God. This is its true glory and source of merit, all the more admirable when we consider the religions of the other peoples of ancient times.

In Egypt and in the countries of Asia around the Mediterranean Sea, and later on in Greece and Rome, people believed in a great number of different gods. Their religion was primitive and outlandish; all the forces of nature were gods: the wind and the rain, thunder, and earthquakes. The heavenly bodies were also gods; people adored the Sun God, the Moon Goddess and innumerable minor star gods. Even animals were adored as gods. In Egypt they venerated the sacred ox; it was a graver crime to kill a cat than to kill a man. Strange idols, half man, half animal, such as the Sphinx, were also worshipped.

The Hebrews, for their part, refused to believe in these absurd gods. "No," they said, "there is but one God! Those divinities you worship are only signs of His power. The forces of nature depend upon His Will. It was He who created the sun, the moon and the stars, just as He has created all living things. It is He who has given life to man, and on earth man can do no better than to know, love and serve Him."

There is the great idea that inspired this small people; there is the reason why the Hebrews deserved the special protection of God, and the reason why their fame is so great. This idea is above all others the message of the Bible, the Book inspired by God Himself. For two thousand years the Hebrew people unceasingly proclaimed their belief in these words and others like them. It often happened that other peoples who believed in numerous false gods tried to force the Hebrews away from their belief in the One True God; they tried to make them worship idols, the images of false gods; but all their efforts were in vain. Many Israelites, in the course of the centuries, laid down their lives for their faith.

It is from this idea, born of a small nation, that our religion has sprung. Many parts of Christian belief come directly from Jewish teaching. When, for example, in the course of your night prayers you recite the words, "I believe in God, the Father Almighty, Creator of heaven and earth," you are repeating a formula first given to the world by the Hebrews. And when you repeat the Commandment, "I am the Lord Thy God; thou shalt not have strange gods before Me," you are quoting what was proclaimed four thousand years ago by the believers of Israel.

Thus we see that the Bible is, above all, God's Book. It speaks of Him and explains how, in the course of centuries, the Jewish nation came to know Him better. It also tells of the struggles and trials the Hebrews had to suffer in order to defend their faith. And it is because this great story is entirely dedicated to the glory of God that we call it Sacred Scripture.

Truly, Israel was a small nation, but it taught the entire world!

II

God's Covenant with Abraham

"ABRAHAM! ABRAHAM!" The young man turned his head several times, for he was alone with his flocks which were grazing along the banks of the Euphrates.

"Abraham! Abraham!" Again came the mysterious voice, loud as thunder but which, instead of frightening him, filled him with joy. "Abraham! Abraham!" Was it but the noise of the wind in the willows or the dull slap of the water against the banks? No! the words were too distinct and each seemed to penetrate to his very heart. Motionless and trembling, the young tribal chief was slow to understand, but the voice continued to call him by name. Finally, the truth dawned on him and he bowed himself down on the ground. "Lord," he whispered, "I am ready to obey. What do you wish me to do?"

God then spoke. "Abraham, I know that you are faithful to Me. You and your people know Me and worship Me. Hear Me: it is not My Will for you to remain longer among the idolatrous people of the Euphrates country. You and your people must depart! Go whither I will lead you. And if you obey Me, I will make you the founder of a great nation and you will be famous forever."

The Voice was stilled. Abraham, standing up, surveyed the plain around him. All was quiet and silent. Hastily he returned to the camp of his kin and told them, "Make haste! Fold the tents and load the donkeys, for we must go. It is the Will of God."

All this took place two thousand years before our era; two thousand years before Jesus Christ appeared on earth, that is, about four thousand years ago (see at end of book note on the counting of dates). At this period of history, the greater portion of the Western world was sunk in barbarism. All Europe was populated by tribes who were less advanced in civilization than the African Negroes of today. But already, in two privileged regions, civilization had been established, and two powerful nations had grown up.

One of these regions was Egypt, of which we have already read. It had been in existence long before the birth of Moses, and even before Abraham. Already for a thousand years it had been a kingdom, well administered under the rule of the Pharaos. Six hundred years earlier the first kings of Egypt had caused to be built those immense tombs, 450 feet high, which we call the Pyramids. The Egyptians were skilled in architecture, sculpture, painting and all the arts. Thanks to the Nile, the country was immensely rich; for every year in the spring this great river overflows its banks and waters its valley. Without the waters of the Nile, Egypt would be nothing more than a desert.

The other civilized nation of the ancient world was Mesopotamia (see map on p. 106), a country in Asia situated not far from the Mediterranean. Here too, the wealth of the country depends on the waters of its rivers: the Tigris and the Euphrates flow down from the mountains, irrigating the land which, once it is sufficiently watered, is wonderfully fertile. Wheat, barley, vines, fruit trees and palms all flourish there, and the pastures are also excellent. Here, as in Egypt, there were organized states, ruled over by powerful kings. For a thousand years, cities had been built there with streets and houses made of brick. Ur, Uruk, and Lagash were among the most important, but they were all surpassed by the riches of Babylon with its palaces famous throughout the ancient world.

Abraham lived in the country round Ur; it was from there that he and his people took their departure on God's command.

It was an animated scene. The donkeys brayed and men shouted instructions and orders. The tents were folded and the carpets rolled up. The women and children packed all their belongings into baskets and bags, while the shepherds gathered their flocks of goats and sheep.

They were off! The Hebrews, as we know, were nomads, making their camps outside city gates and having little to do with the citizens. They could therefore move quickly, and such a move surprised no one, for people were used to it. On the desert routes one often came across such caravans of asses (horses were unknown in the region), whole tribes on the move in the search for new pastures for their herds. Abraham and his kinsmen mounted their camels and slowly, in a long column, the tribe headed toward the north.

Abraham left no one behind; neither his old father Thare, nor his wife Sara, nor his nephew Lot. Everyone, friends and servants alike, embarked on the adventure, and it was from these close associates of Abraham that the chosen people were born. Where were they going? Even the leader himself did not know; he knew only that the first stage of the journey would lead to Haran, at the foot of the Taurus mountains. That was a long way, almost eight hundred miles from Ur. But we do not need to ask questions when God is our guide, nor does one feel fatigue when on the march toward a great destiny.

Haran was only a halting place, for the land which God intended for the Hebrews was much farther off. Always obedient to the commands of the Lord, Abraham set forth again, facing south this time (see map on front endpaper) in the direction of the Land of Chanaan.

The Land of Chanaan! How many times will this name appear in our story, for Chanaan, which we call Palestine, was the country chosen by God for the Hebrews; the stage on which would be played the great drama of their history; the beloved home for which they would sigh when they were exiled from it. Today, and ever since Christ dwelt there, we call it the *Holy Land.* But, the Hebrews asked themselves, how could they, a wandering, helpless people, worn out after an interminable journey, secure and hold for themselves this land that God had promised them?

Happily for them, God was watching over them.

Once again, God spoke to His faithful servant. "You have been obedient to My commands, Abraham. You left the land of the idolators in order to keep your people from the worship of false gods. You have believed in Me; and your people, alone among the peoples of the world, know that I exist, that I am the sole Master of heaven and earth, and they alone obey My Will. So it is that your fidelity shall have its reward. This country to which you have come shall belong to your descendants, to the great nation that shall be born of you. Better still, there shall be established between us a Covenant that shall last forever."

A Covenant! What could be more astonishing than that God should ally Himself to a people.

"You shall be My witness upon earth. You will teach other men all that they must know about Me. In return, as long as you and your descendants remain faithful to me, I will give to you My special protection. I will make your enemies fall before you, and I will lead you to immortal glory."

This was the meaning of the words spoken by God, and we can well imagine the joy Abraham felt at hearing them. One thing, however, worried him. The Lord had told him that he would have many descendants, but how could this come to be, since his wife and he had no children? Many years had passed since the tribe had started on its voyage from Ur and, by the time it was settled in Chanaan, Abraham was almost ninety years old.

God knew his fears on this point and said to him, "Look up to the heavens and number the stars, if you can. So shall your children be."

Some little time later, one fine, warm spring day, as Abraham was taking his ease at the door of his tent in the shade of some oak trees, three strangers came to him and asked for refreshment.

He gave this generously, offering his guests a fine roast of veal and fresh cakes. These three strangers were angels, sent by God to give Abraham the good news that soon he would have a son.

True to this promise, Sara, his wife, had a little boy some months later. He was named Isaac, which in the Hebrew language means something like "joyous laughter," for we can well imagine how the coming of their little son delighted Abraham and Sara who had waited so long for a child.

So did God show His power to keep the promise he had made to His faithful followers. At the same time, He was to give another and a very terrible proof.

Not far from where Abraham and his household had pitched their tents, lay the Jordan Valley, a lovely pattern of rich pasture and well-tilled fields. There were two splendid towns there: Sodom and Gomorrah. But alas, their inhabitants, although rich, led very bad lives. There was no sin that they did not commit, and again and again God had warned them to mend their ways. His warnings were all in vain, and in the two cities there was only one family that led a virtuous life: that of Abraham's nephew, Lot, who had settled there.

Finally, God's patience was exhausted. He decided that the sinful cities must perish, and He released against them the fearful powers of the elements. The earth shook, and fire from heaven rained down on the doomed towns, destroying crops, pastures and woods, and reducing the houses to ashes. In fact, what happened was a violent and terrible volcanic eruption.

Today, when we travel in Palestine we may visit the site of these ill-fated cities. We find there now, in a depression so deep that it lies nearly thirteen hundred feet below the level of the Mediterranean, a strange expanse of water so salty and so dense that the human body cannot sink in it. As we approach, we are struck by the fact that no living thing is to be found on the banks of this mournful lake; not a bird, not even a plant. This is the Dead Sea, an enduring reminder of the anger of God.

As for Lot, God had no cause for anger against him, and he was warned in good time of the approaching disaster. "Go," God told him, "and take with you your wife and two daughters so that you may not perish. But remember this: for no reason whatsoever are any of you to look backward in your flight, no one should see the horrors that are to come." It happened, however, that Lot's wife—you know what people say about the curiosity of woman!—could not resist a backward glance, and instantly she was turned into a pillar of salt.

In the desolate district around the Dead Sea, one can still see great blocks of salt which look like white statues of human beings, fixed there forever by the anger of God.

While all these events were taking place, little Isaac was growing up and he became the joy of his parents' life. He was about fifteen years of age when again the Voice of God called to his father:

"Abraham! Abraham!"

"Here I am, O Lord!"

"Take your beloved son Isaac up to a high mountain, and there offer him to Me in sacrifice."

Abraham must have been overwhelmed at this terrible command. But not for an instant did he think of disobeying it. He loaded a donkey with wood faggots and, calling Isaac, he led him toward the mountain of Moria. As they were on the way, the child said to him, "Father, I see that we are bringing the wood for a burnt sacrifice, but where is the victim?" Poor Abraham hardly knew how to reply.

We must explain here that throughout the countries from Palestine to Mesopotamia it was customary for idolatrous peoples to offer as sacrifices to their false gods not merely animals such as sheep or cattle, but also human beings. Here and there on mountain tops have been found the bones of many poor people who were thus sacrificed to cruel gods. But all the same it was a very strange thing that God, the True God, should ask for so horrible a thing!

When they had climbed up the mountain, Abraham prepared the wood for his fire and, seizing his son, tied him to it. But, just at the moment he was raising his knife to slay the child, an angel held

back his arm. Looking around him he saw a ram tied to a nearby bush ready for sacrifice. Then the Voice of God came to him:

"Abraham, this was but a test. You did not hesitate to sacrifice to Me your only son, and that is enough. Sacrifice this ram in the place of the child. Now I know that of all those who serve Me, you are the most faithful. I will bless you, and your descendants will be countless as the stars of heaven and the sands that are on the sea shore."

This was the last great event of Abraham's very eventful life. His closing years were spent in peace and quiet, while around him a more and more numerous nation began to grow. He was hailed as the patriarch, the father of all, the venerated ancestor. When at last he died, he was one hundred and seventy-five years old!

III

Romance and Adventure in the Days of Isaac and Jacob

ONE OF THE MOST DIFFICULT MATTERS in life is to make a successful and happy marriage, and for a man to choose a wife who is both attractive and serious-minded; one who will be a true companion in good times and bad, one who will be a good housekeeper and an excellent mother for his future children. It is no easy task to find such a woman, and one cannot give too much attention to his search.

Some such thoughts as these were occupying Isaac's mind. He had grown to manhood well before his father's death and so he confided to Abraham his wish to get married. Since none of the girls of his own tribe pleased him sufficiently, what, he asked, was he to do?

"Whatever else you do," replied the wise old patriarch, "you must not marry a foreigner, a woman from the towns of Chanaan whose people worship idols and do not know the True God. You must find as wife one of our own race. I'll see what I can do about it."

Abraham then sent for the most trusted of his servants and told him, "You must go to the land where our fathers used to live, to the country of Haran and the land of the great rivers. Many of our people and our friends still dwell there. From among them you will choose a wife for my son. She must be pretty and pleasant, but above all, she must be good and loyal, one who could become an ideal wife."

The servant set out on his way with a small caravan of ten camels. He took with him a magnificent set of jewelry: necklace, ring and bracelets all of solid gold, to offer the young girl he would choose. But, as he went his way he began to wonder to himself, "How can I make sure that she is good and loyal and that she has all the qualities they wish?"

Then an idea struck him. Having reached the Euphrates country, he took up a place beside a well as though he were a tired and thirsty traveler who had no vessel in which to draw water. In the East to this day you can see women coming in long files to the well to draw water, each with a pitcher balanced on her head—a graceful sight. Abraham's messenger knew that many women would come to the well, but none of those who did so offered him a drink from her pitcher.

Finally, there drew near one young girl, beautiful and fair of face. Her pitcher was so perfectly balanced on her lovely head that you would have thought she was carrying it for amusement.

She had filled her pitcher and was about to go away when she noticed the stranger. She at once asked him if he was thirsty and would he like her to draw some water for him? When he said he would like a drink, she hastened to pour for him all he wanted to slake his thirst, and then she asked about his camels. Had they had a drink after their long journey? Learning that they had not, she drew bucket after bucket to fill the trough so that the good and tireless beasts could quench their thirst.

The servant now realized that God Himself had sent this unknown girl to him and that he need look no further. A young girl who showed such kindness to a stranger and his beasts could but possess the finest qualities of character. When asked her name, she said, "Rebecca."—Rebecca!

It was clear that God Himself had brought about this meeting, for Rebecca belonged to the Hebrew people and was actually a distant relative of Isaac's.

Bowing low before the surprised girl, the faithful servant presented her with the ring, the necklace, and the bracelets, and begged her to lead him to her father.

And so it was that Isaac married Rebecca.

When Abraham died, Isaac took his place as chief of the tribe. Just before his father had closed his eyes forever, he had blessed him, calling down upon his head the protection of God. In his turn, therefore, and for many long years, Isaac ruled as patriarch, respected by all and loved by all as a father, so that he had scarcely the need to give an order to have his wishes carried out.

Let us try to picture for ourselves the sort of life led by the Hebrews at this period. They had settled themselves in Chanaan, but merely as birds of passage. They did not dwell in the towns. These belonged to other peoples who were long established in the country, people called Chanaanites and Hethites, who were of course idolators, and therefore distrusted by the Hebrews. God's people continued to live as nomads, following their herds about the country which was easy for them to do as, in order to move, all they had to do was to fold their tents. Isaac did teach them to dig many wells and to grow some wheat.

How simple life was in the days of the Patriarchs, with no houses or furniture to tie people down! Food was simple and healthy: mostly bread, milk, cheese and honey; and at night they slept on a carpet or matting. In the evenings, at the hour when the Eastern sky becomes the color of pearl, the people gathered round their tents and sat cross-legged on the ground to listen to the old men repeating in long poetic narratives of wondrous beauty the traditions that had been handed down from generation to generation from the beginning of time.

Religion, too, was very simple. They prayed to God and avoided idols, and on feast days they sacrificed the finest lamb of the flock in honor of the Most High. And sometimes, to mark the spot where the people had called on God for help, they erected a stone as a sort of monument, usually on the summit of a high mountain overlooking the wide plains below. And that was all.

Later in their history, when the Hebrews had grown rich and had settled in towns and on farms and were bound by complicated laws, they looked back with regret to the time they lived in tents. For it is in poverty and simplicity that we come closest to God.

Now Isaac and Rebecca had two sons, Esau and Jacob, who, although they were brothers, differed greatly from each other. Esau was a sturdy and vigorous youth, hairy and red, while Jacob was a fine boy, slender and well built. Esau was only interested in physical prowess—hunting and warfare—and spent most of his time high up in the mountains. Jacob was a peaceable young man, a good shepherd for the flocks. It was not surprising that the two, so different in character, did not always get on well with each other. Rebecca showed a marked preference for Jacob, but Isaac, who in his old age had become very fond of food, favored Esau because he brought home tasty pieces of game for the pot.

Esau was the older of the two brothers, which meant that, on his father's death, he would succeed him as leader of the tribe. Now, one day when Esau returned tired out from hunting, he found his brother preparing a fine meal outside his tent. A dish of lentils was simmering away, and it had a delicious smell. (I expect that in it was a good-sized piece of tender goat meat, for this is a dish that they prepare in the East to this day.)

"Let me have a mouthful of your food," Esau asked his brother.

"Only on condition that you give up your birthright," replied Jacob. This meant that on the death of their father, Esau would allow Jacob to succeed Isaac as leader.

Esau, who was famished, was forced to agree to Jacob's terms. And perhaps, you may say, they were not very generous or charitable. But, when you hear what followed, you will understand why God allowed these things to happen.

Some time later, Esau married and, instead of choosing young Hebrew girls, he married foreigners, town dwellers, who were of course idolators. (I use the word "girls," because it was the custom of the Hebrews at that time, as it is the custom of the Arabs to-day, to have several wives.) You can imagine how Esau's choice distressed his parents. Rebecca was so upset that she declared, "I would rather die than see my Jacob marry women like that." She then began to plan that Esau would not succeed his father as patriarch.

Esau's surrender of his birthright was not enough to make Jacob the rightful heir; this had to be confirmed by his father. One day the aged Isaac, who was by now blind and who felt that he was soon to die, called Esau to him.

"You are my first born," he said, "and I am going to give you my blessing, but first of all, go hunting and bring back a good bag of game."

Rebecca heard what Isaac had said and, while Esau was away at the hunt, she made haste to cook a hare in the way the old man liked it best. She then called Jacob and made him wrap his hands and arms in the skin of a goat, so that were one to touch him he

would feel hairy like his brother. Jacob took Esau's place and offered the dish to his father. Isaac, mistaking him for Esau, blessed him and named him as his heir. When the hunter returned from the chase, he found that he had been displaced.

So it was that Jacob succeeded Isaac; partly because his mother willed it so, but above all to teach the Hebrews not to mix by marriage with the idolatrous peoples of Chanaan.

You can imagine Esau's anger at the trick that had been played on him. It was so violent that Jacob, who was much smaller than his brother, decided that it would be more prudent for him to go away. On his mother's advice, he left for the land of his ancestors, that district of Haran from which Rebecca had come. There, he felt sure, he would find a worthy wife.

He departed therefore for the north, saddened at having to leave home, and not knowing when he would be able to return. God, however, was watching over him and did not wish him to be troubled. One night, as he was sleeping in the open under the stars, a dream came to him. In it he beheld a great ladder reaching from earth to heaven, up and down which angels passed in an unending procession. God Himself was enthroned at the top of the ladder and, in his dream, Jacob heard a mighty Voice.

"I am the Lord God, the God of Abraham, and the God of Isaac. The land whereon you now sleep shall one day be the country of your descendants. They shall be countless, glorious and blessed. As for yourself, you are under My protection; you will return safe and sound to your own country. Fear not, for you are in no danger."

When Jacob awoke he was comforted and in good spirits for his journey. On the spot where the dream came to him, he erected a monument which he called Bethel, that is, "the House of God." Then he continued on his way to the north.

When he reached the region of the Two Rivers he met his cousin Rachael, the daughter of his mother's brother, and she was so beautiful that at once he wished to marry her. Rachel, however, had a sister, Lia, who was as plain as Rachel was pretty. When he asked to marry Rachel, the girls' father told Jacob that he would only give his consent if he married both of them. So it was that Jacob found himself with two wives and, in time, a fine family of no less than twelve sons.

Jacob stayed for a long while in Haran—twenty years in fact, the Bible tells us—working for his father-in-law, guarding his flocks and building a comfortable fortune for himself. But he never forgot that he was Isaac's heir and that back in Chanaan his old blind father, his beloved mother, and all his people awaited him. One day he decided to return to them.

This journey was not without its anxieties. Jacob knew that Esau had said, "If he returns, I will kill him!" On the road back Jacob constantly prayed to God, "O, my God, God of my fathers, I am Thy servant and I know that I am under Thy protection. Nevertheless, I greatly fear the anger of Esau. Since you have promised me that my descendants shall rule the land, come Thou to my aid. Do not allow me to perish!"

The nearer he came to Chanaan, the more he was filled with doubts and fear. He had been absent for twenty years; would his tribe still accept him as their leader? And was he himself worthy to be the leader of God's people? One evening he had almost decided to halt and turn back. But that night, he was again visited by a dream. In it he found himself struggling with a being of enormous strength who forced him to continue the task which he had been about to abandon, and this being was one of God's angels. When Jacob awoke, worn out as though he had actually been in a battle, he realized the meaning of the dream: the Will of the Lord God must not be opposed. It was after this dream that Jacob took the surname Israel, which means, "he who prevailed with God"; and later this name came to be applied to all his people.

In the end, things turned out very well. Esau, pleased at receiving handsome presents, did not show such great hostility. Jacob arrived home in time to see his old father before the latter died. He ordered the destruction of the idols which some wicked people among the Hebrews had set up and adored during his absence. Under his rule as patriarch the old simple and contented way of life continued, the way of life of a good people who enjoyed the protection of God.

IV

What the Old Hebrews Told of the Beginning of the World and of Man

PERHAPS while you were reading these pages you have wondered what were the great stories told by the old men of the tribe in the evenings when the sun was descending into the purple of the Mediterranean and the smoke of the camp fires rose into the still, pure air. I will tell you these stories, for we know them very well; it was God's Will that they should be included in the Bible, and they form the first chapters of that holy Book which was inspired by Him. They are wonderful stories, full of interest for us, for what those old poets of nomadic days had to tell was nothing less than the history of the World and of Man, the sacred epic of the Creation.

Try to imagine for yourself these old poets. Surrounded by a circle of silent listeners, they chanted their words in a singing voice. They could keep up their recitations forever, for they knew their subject by heart, and indeed it was in order to help their memory that the text of the Bible is divided into verses and stanzas, with repetitions.

The art of writing was known at this period. It had been discovered at about the same time both in Egypt and Mesopotamia, at least six centuries before the time of Abraham. But the mode of writing in use around the Euphrates, the only one known to the Hebrews, was not a very convenient one, as it was engraved on bricks. While the clay was still soft, characters were engraved on it with a metal tool, and the brick was then left to harden in the sun. This type of writing was known as "cuneiform" and, while it had the advantage of being indelible, the tablets or bricks were heavy and not easy to handle. One can hardly imagine Abraham and his people starting off on their travels from Ur with their asses laden with a library of bricks!

So it was that the traditions of the Hebrews were stored in the human memory. They were trained from infancy to memorize very long texts and were able to repeat these for hours at a time without ever making a mistake. All the nomadic peoples, such as the Arabs, for instance, could do the same. Thus the ancient traditions were handed down from father to son, from teacher to pupil, from generation to generation through the long centuries. The text of the Bible was preserved in this manner for, as we shall see, it was only at a much later period that it was put down in writing.

Let us listen then to these remote narrators of the Hebrew people as though we were really sitting at their feet. Let us hear them with respect and belief, for what they tell us, however extraordinary it may seem to us, is certainly true, since it was revealed to man by God Himself. This is what they told:

In the beginning of all things, the earth was in a state of terrible disorder and confusion. Somewhere in the mighty universe our world was a tiny sphere, shapeless and empty. But God was watching, and decided to impose His order on all that already existed through His Will.

"Be light made," He said, and there was light.—"Let the light of day be separated from the darkness of the night." And it was so.—"Let the waters and the land be separated." And the oceans took their places and the continents displayed their vast expanses. —"Let the light of the heaven fall upon the earth and illuminate it." And in the mighty vault of heaven appeared the sun, the moon and the stars. . . .

So it was that the earth was made ready to receive living beings. The next task that God set Himself was the creation of these. At His Word, the seas were filled with countless fishes and the air with the wings of birds. There appeared on the earth every kind of living thing known to us, not merely those we deem useful to us, but those whose purpose we do not understand but which most certainly have their own place in the Divine Plan.

When all the animals had been created, God decided to create a living being more perfect than them all, who would be endowed with wonderful gifts: intelligence, the power of speech, a language, and a pair of hands capable of all necessary tasks. He took a piece of earth, good fertile clay such as one finds in the plain between the Two Rivers, and fashioned it to his idea, making a sort of statue in the shape of a man, but without life. Then He gently breathed through the nostrils of this lifeless image and, at once, the statue opened its eyes and became alive.

So, in His bounty, God Himself created the world, the earth, and all living things, including man—working day after day like a good craftsman. And on the seventh day, again like a good workman, God rested and looked over His work. He found it good and well made. And this was true: the world *is* beautiful, when it is not spoiled by the ugliness and malice of man.

The first man was called Adam, and God had made him to His own image and likeness; that is to say that he had an immortal soul, he was able to understand many things and to distinguish between good and evil. Picture, if you can, this first man in all his wonderful youth and strength, born of the hands of the Creator, and destined to rule the world in the name of God. What a marvelous life lay before him and how happy he should have been!

God had made him the master of all living things. All the fruits of the trees and of the soil were at his service. He knew neither the hunger or cold which today cause so much suffering to men. Best of all, he did not have to die. He was immortal, like God Himself.

This first man passed his days of happiness in a garden which God had made to bloom especially for him. This garden was called "Paradise" or the "Garden of Eden." The trees in it produced only the most delicious fruits, as pleasant to look at as they were to eat. The clear waters of the rivers that flowed through it gave it a perfect climate and fertility. Adam was set there as the most honored of guests, and caring for the beautiful garden was but a pastime for him. . . .

To complete his happiness and to save him from being lonely, God provided Adam with a companion. One day, when the first man was asleep in the open air, the Creator took from his chest a portion of his flesh; from this rib He shaped a woman and He gave her to Adam. She was called Eve and Adam loved her. Thenceforth they lived together: theirs was the first marriage, and they the first man and woman on earth. From them every human being is descended.

Everything was perfect in Paradise and if man had remained obedient to God, he would have stayed there forever.

Alas, this wonderful state of happiness was not to last. . . . It must be explained that at the same time He created man, God gave life to other beings, the angels. They were more beautiful and perfect than man. They had no body, only a spirit, a soul, with which they could know God. The angels do not usually appear on earth, except when God sends them here on some special mission. Their duty is to praise God in heaven and to sing of His virtues, His goodness and His power.

But the angels were just as capable as man of doing wrong. One of them thought himself so beautiful, so clever and so perfect that he fell victim to the sin of pride. He actually thought himself the equal of God, and one day he rebelled against the Lord God. He was, of course, defeated and cast out of Heaven. He was condemned, with all the wicked angels who supported him, to dwell forever in a bottomless pit.

This dark angel was called Lucifer, or Satan, and his accomplices became devils. They had a fierce hatred for God and tried always to have revenge on Him, as though such creatures could prevail against their Creator! Failing to overcome God, they now assailed man, and this was the beginning of the latter's misfortune.

Satan came to earth and took the appearance of the serpent, the wiliest of all the animals. In order to injure God, would it not be a good plan to encourage Adam to rebel against Him?

Among the trees in Paradise, there was one very mysterious one which God had forbidden Adam to touch. "Eat the fruit of all the trees as you wish, except this one," God had told him. "For, if you eat of this, you will die." The name of the tree was "the Tree of Knowledge of Good and Evil" which is, as you see, a very mysterious name.

The serpent now made his way toward the humans. He found Eve alone in a grove in the lovely garden. In those days there was no hatred between humans and animals, and so Eve was not frightened and did not cry for help as one of her descendants would certainly do if a huge snake tried to talk to her.

"Is it true," the tempter asked her, "that you are denied the right to eat the fruits of all the trees here?"

"Yes," said Eve, "there is one tree whose fruit we are forbidden to touch, the Tree of the Knowledge of Good and Evil."

The serpent hissed sneeringly. "And do you know why God has forbidden you to touch it? It is because whoever eats it himself becomes God. He is able to see all things, to do all things and to understand all things. Now you know the reason why this old Master of yours is jealous of His authority and has forbidden you this fruit, the choicest of all on earth. It is because He fears that you would dethrone Him. If I were you, I would try a taste."

Women, we are told, are prone to curiosity. Once the serpent had spoken, Eve could not restrain hers. She stretched out toward the fruit, hesitated a moment, drew back her hand and then hastily seized the fruit and took a bite from it. At this moment Adam arrived on the scene. At first he was very angry with his wife for her disobedience, but she insisted so much, and spoke so glowingly of the delicious flavor and delicate perfume of the fruit that he too let himself be tempted. And thus took place man's first act of disobedience to God, his first sin.

God knows all things, and nothing that man does is overlooked by Him. The most perfect of his earthly creatures had disobeyed Him and so, the great Voice called out, "Where are you, Adam?" Adam was slow to reply, for by this time he realized his fault and he was ashamed. You may think that it was not after all such a very terrible sin to eat a piece of fruit, even if it *did* come from such a mysterious tree. But the serious thing was that Adam had disobeyed his Master, and had destroyed the pact of trust that up to now had existed between them.

At length Adam replied tremblingly, "Here I am, Lord."

"What have you done that you are so ashamed?"

"Eve gave me fruit from the forbidden tree, and I allowed myself to eat it."

The earth trembled and there was a deafening peal of thunder as the anger of the Lord God broke forth. "Since you have disobeyed My orders, you must now suffer the consequence of your sin. From now on, life for you in Paradise, the Garden of Delight, is over. You will have to labor hard in order to live: you will earn your bread in the sweat of your brow. Suffering and hatred, injustice and violence will be your lot in this life, and in the end death, which I had intended to spare you, will come to you and you will return to the dust from which I created you."

When God had ceased to speak, an angel shining in light and carrying a fiery sword, appeared before the stricken Adam. Bent double beneath the weight of their shame and despair, the man and the woman fled from the garden where they had been so happy and which they had lost through their sin. When they had left, the angel remained on guard before the gate, the flaming sword in his hand.

This is the way the ancient Hebrews tell of the beginning of man and it explains why there is so much grandeur in him: because he was the chosen creature of God. It also explains why there is so much misery in life: because man sinned against God.

V

The Story Continued: The Wickedness of Man and the Anger of God

"SUFFERING AND HATRED, violence and injustice, shall be the lot of man. . . ." Alas, the sentence pronounced by God was quickly fulfilled and we see the results of it still. How many crimes, how many horrible deeds have been committed by man since the moment when, through Adam's disobedience, evil first made its appearance on earth! You can see for yourself how right the old Hebrew narrators were when they blamed man's sin for everything that went wrong in this world. Had we remained in the Garden of Eden we would never have known wars, misery, famine or death. . . .

Now let us continue the Bible story of the beginnings of mankind. As you will see, even in those far-off days, man was not a very lovable being.

Following their marriage, Adam and Eve had two children, both boys: one was called Cain and the other Abel. Cain tilled the fields and Abel guarded the flocks. They did not get on well together, or rather Abel, who was an upright and pleasant lad, felt nothing but affection for his brother. But Cain detested Abel. Why? Probably because he was jealous. To be sure it is a hard task to be a tiller of the soil: it means getting up at dawn and working all day in the sun or the rain, and not getting home until nightfall, tired and worn out. By comparison, the life of a shepherd seems an easy one—it seems to take no great effort to keep watch over the beasts as they graze. All the same, it is a tiring enough task to follow the goats and the sheep all day to prevent them from straying, and to stay awake at night lest the flocks be attacked by wolves.

Be that as it may, Cain *was* jealous of Abel. When he made sacrifice to God of the fruits of his labors he kept telling himself of the work it had cost him to grow them; whereas when Abel offered up a lamb, the sacrifice had cost him little. God Himself, who reads the heart of man, had warned Cain that jealousy was a bad counselor and would lead him into sin, but Cain would not listen. As he dug and weeded and hoed the land, he nursed his hate in secret.

One day, in a state of furious anger, he met Abel and killed him with a blow. Instantly the Voice of God came to him.

"Cain, where is your brother Abel?"

The terrified murderer stammered and tried to lie. "I know not. Am I my brother's keeper?"

The Voice of the Almighty replied, "Wretched man, what have you done? Your brother's blood cries out to Me from the earth. Flee, if you can. For now you are accursed, you who have watered the earth with the first human blood. Henceforth you shall be a wanderer across the face of the earth, a fugitive never finding peace thereon."

As it was with Cain, so has it been ever since with men who have committed great crimes. In vain they seek refuge in flight, in hiding, in going from country to country; wherever they go an all-powerful force pursues and accompanies them. They can never escape from it, for it is part of themselves; it is the voice of conscience which forever reminds them of their wrong-doing.

At the death of Abel his father and mother were overcome by grief. For the first time human beings had seen the death of one they loved and, worse still, one son had been the murderer of his brother. It was truly dreadful, but God had pity on the unhappy parents and He sent Eve another son to take Abel's place. She called him Seth, which in Hebrew means "the replacement." Seth, like his dead brother, was a pleasant and kind-hearted boy.

The entire human race is thus descended from Seth and from Cain, and that is why there are always good people and wicked people in the world. To this day, we find people who are full of charity and goodwill toward their neighbors and others who carry hatred and violence in their hearts. It is not pleasant to have to admit it, but this has been the way since man first came into the world.

Adam's descendants grew quickly in number. His sons had large families, and before long there emerged the first craftsmen. In addition to the farmers and the shepherds there appeared the blacksmiths, the potters, the carpenters and others like them; there soon appeared the first artists, and musicians who played on the harp and the reed pipe.

These first human beings were, of course, mortal just as we are, since God had decreed that, in punishment for Adam's sin, man must suffer death. Their lives were, however, much longer than ours. Adam lived for no less than 930 years which, we must admit, was a fine long life. His son Seth lived to be 912, and Seth's son to the age of 905. . . . Their ages seem extraordinary to us, but the Bible tells us of one of Seth's descendants who lived to an even greater age: Mathusala lived to be 969 years old! (This is why even today when we speak of a very old man, we say, "he is as old as Mathusala.")

The Providence of God, which had granted man such a long span of life, did not, however, make his lot easier. The more men multiplied, the worse they became, and the more their deeds of violence and jealousy increased. The different tribes fought with each other over the pastures for their herds, and the farmers stole one another's crops. Wars broke out and, with the bronze weapons they already knew how to make, the descendants of Adam were already killing each other in armed conflict. It seemed as though man was using the intelligence given to him by the Creator only for evil purposes.

Finally, the Lord God repented that He had ever created such a brood. "Since the world is given over to wickedness, I shall destroy it and every human being on it!" He said.

So He sent the Deluge, and we will now tell the story of it.

Rain! Rain! A terrible and unending downpour. Across a black, forbidding sky raced towering clouds driven by an unceasing wind. Rain! Rain! Still it poured down on woods and fields, on mountains and valleys, until it numbed the minds and sickened the hearts of men. Still more rain, until the rivers were unable to carry the floods to the sea, and the drenched soil could absorb no more water. Gradually the flood rose and deepened until it covered everything, and the rivers, lakes, seas and oceans became one. This was no normal rain; it was an unimaginable disaster, the Deluge decreed by the Lord God.

Men fled in terror from the plains. They climbed to the hills and then to the mountains. Their efforts to escape were all in vain, for the floods rose too quickly for them. This terrible rainfall lasted for forty days and forty nights, and when it was over the whole surface of the earth was one immense sea, disturbed only by sullen waves, the true reflection of the anger of God.

(In our own time, scientists who have studied the ancient civilizations of Mesopotamia have made some interesting discoveries on the subject of the Deluge. In going through the inscriptions left by other peoples who dwelt in the Euphrates country, such as the Chaldeans and the Assyrians, they found that these too knew of a deluge and had left records of it. So once again we find that the old traditions of the Hebrew people are perfectly true.)

But what is this strange object that we see drifting before the wind on this mighty sea? It looks like a ship, and a big one, completely closed up and with no sign of a crew. And that is exactly what it is: a boat with human beings inside it who have taken shelter there and who now await the end of the disaster.

Among all the wicked people who inhabited the earth there had been one exception. Noe was an upright, honest, and good man. God had decided to spare him. Warning him in advance of the disaster that was about to befall the world, He ordered Noe to make a ship, an Ark so sturdily built that it would resist the waves and the tempest.

It was this Ark, built of sound timber and caulked with tar, that now bore Noe and saved him from certain death. God had allowed him to take his entire family on board with him and also a pair of every species of animal. What a fine floating zoo the Ark must have been! Noe could watch from a porthole all that went on outside the ship.

When the forty days had passed, it appeared to the passengers in the Ark that the tempest was dying away. They sent forth a dove to find out what conditions were like outside. Toward evening the bird returned, carrying a fresh twig of olive in its beak. Noe understood from this that some portion of the earth must now be above the waters. He steered the Ark toward a high mountain in the Caucasus called Ararat (see map on p. 106). Here he cast anchor and disembarked all his passengers, human and animal.

And so it was that by the goodness of God the world was peopled once more. From Noe and his family came a new race of men, and from each pair of animals he had embarked on the Ark, a race of animals. Life commenced once more. Noe guided his family, which soon became a very large one, with great wisdom. It was he who taught men how to cultivate the vine. But in his heart he always dreaded the coming of another Deluge, and he prayed to God not to let it happen again.

God gave Noe the promise he asked. In proof of His friendship for Noe, His faithful servant, He pledged Himself never again to destroy the entire human race, and to show pity even if men behaved badly. And as a token of His forgiveness and renewed friendship with man, He set a rainbow in the sky—the rainbow which, as you know, marks the end of a storm and is a sign of good weather to come.

Grown men can be very like children: when the head of the house is angry, they behave themselves, but as soon as he is appeased, they begin again to do as they please. As time passed by, Noe's descendants began to forget the Deluge and the fearful punishment that God had inflicted on their ancestors. They went back to their old quarrelsome and violent ways, lied, and did injustice one to the other. In addition, they grew haughty and thought in their foolish minds they could equal the Lord!

Because of their pride, they now undertook a ridiculous scheme. They had discovered in the plain between the Two Rivers that was called Mesopotamia, at a place called Babel (later to be named Babylon), a type of clay that made excellent bricks, and with these bricks they had learned to build houses. So far so good, but now some of them proposed a crazy plan. "Let us," they said, "build a great tower with our bricks, a tower higher than any monument or mountain on earth, a tower that will reach up to heaven itself." What nonsense to imagine that they could build from earth to heaven!

And so the poor vain fools set to work, and made huge piles of bricks. The tower was built one story upon the other, each a bit smaller than the one below it, so that the effect was rather that of a pyramid. And between the different stories there were ramps, so that even carts could travel up.

(We must tell you here that scientists in our own times have discovered the remains of towers of this type in the Mesopotamian plain; the Chaldeans and the Assyrians built the temples of their idols on the same plan. And when the Hebrews later on described this monument to their own foolish pride, they had in mind those idolatrous temples which, as we know, they held in horror.)

As the tower of Babel grew higher it grew more and more unsafe, but nevertheless the work went on. God decided to punish the builders for their sin of pride, and He did so in a very curious way. Up to that period all men spoke the same language, being all descended from the same ancestor, Noe. Now God made it so that the people could no longer understand each other. Each spoke his own tongue, and no one knew what anyone else was saying. The result was such confusion that the different nations parted very quickly. They could not understand each other's language and each was ready to hate the other. The tower of Babel was never finished, and little by little the wind and the rain and the passing of time reduced it to a ruin. Nothing remained of it except a grass-grown and shapeless pile of bricks.

Such were the grand old traditions handed down to the Hebrew poets of nomadic times, and told by them round the evening camp fires. They explain many things that otherwise we should never be able to understand. That is why we read and believe what is told to us in the first chapters of the Bible.

After the confusion of tongues at Babel, humanity became divided into three groups which, in time, formed the three great races of mankind. Each of these groups took the name of one of Noe's three sons: Sem, Cham and Japheth. Sem's descendents became the Semites and we saw on page 7 that the Hebrew people were an offshoot of the Semite race. This is all very clear and logical. It was some ten generations after the dispersion of the races that Abraham was born and the history of the Hebrew people began.

VI

Joseph's Adventures in the Land of Egypt

NOW LET US GO BACK to the story of our Patriarchs. As you remember, Jacob had twelve sons, a fine family, but large families were usual in those far-off days. Jacob dearly loved all his twelve boys, but it must be admitted that he showed a special preference for one of them, Joseph, because he reminded him so much of his beloved wife Rachel who had died shortly before.

Apart from this, Joseph was such a handsome, refined and intelligent lad that his father's preference for him was quite natural. Jewish children often display an intelligence which is in advance of their age. Jacob spoiled his favorite a little, making him a present of a fine coat of many colors which aroused the envy of the boy's brothers.

For his part, it must be admitted that Joseph did nothing to make their envy less. On the contrary, he was inclined to be somewhat boastful. He used, for instance, to tell of remarkable dreams which came to him.

"I dreamed," he said, "that we were all gathering the harvest together. The sheaf that I had bound was heavier and finer than all the others; it stood erect right in the middle of the field and all the other sheaves bowed down before it."

His brothers laughed at him and asked him the meaning of the dream.

"It means that I shall be your leader, your master, and that you will have to bow down before me."

You can imagine how this endeared Joseph to his brothers!

One day, when Jacob's flocks were grazing far away in the

mountains, the patriarch thought they were delaying too long and sent Joseph to tell his brothers to drive them home.

As he came in sight, one of the brothers cried out, "Here comes the dreamer of dreams!"

"The vain braggart," said another.

"Let us do away with him," suggested a third.

"That would not be difficult in these wild mountains; we can say he was slain by a lion."

The eldest brother, Ruben, was the only one who objected. "No," he said, "we must not stain our hands with our brother's blood. I agree that we must get rid of this conceited babbler, but we must do so without killing him. Let us seize him and sell him into slavery. We will sprinkle the fine coat he is so proud of with the blood of a kid, and bring it back to our father so that he will think that Joseph has been devoured by a wild beast. And if we keep our secret, who is going to learn the truth?"

No sooner said than done. When Joseph joined his brothers they fell upon him, roped him like a beast at a fair and, to make sure that he would not escape, they lowered him to the bottom of an empty water well. As for poor Jacob, when he was shown the bloodstained coat he believed everything that was told him. He was in despair at having sent his beloved son to his death under the lion's claws and, putting on mourning garments, he wept bitterly and long.

Meanwhile a caravan happened to pass close by the well where the unfortunate Joseph had been abandoned. The people of the caravan were desert folk akin to the Bedouins of our time, who followed the trade routes all over Western Asia and were not above a little banditry at times. Joseph's guilty brothers offered him to them as a slave at a very low price. The nomads were glad to accept such a bargain, and they took Joseph with them, intending to resell him elsewhere.

They were on their way to Egypt. There many such caravans used to go, bringing Mesopotamian merchandise to the land of the Nile and returning to the Euphrates with Egyptian products.

When Joseph was offered for sale in the slave market—for in those days men were sold in markets as pigs and sheep are sold today—the captain of the king's army, who was called Putiphar, and who was a very important personage indeed, happened to pass by. Struck by the fine appearance and lively intelligence of the youth, he bought him and took him as a slave to the palace.

On the whole as things turned out, Joseph, in spite of his misfortunes, had still been lucky. He might have been killed, but he was not. He might have fallen into the hands of a cruel master and forced to do hard and tiring work. Nothing of the sort happened, for very soon Putiphar developed a great liking for his young slave and made him his majordomo, that is, he allowed him to manage the entire household in complete liberty.

Truly, God had protected Joseph and indeed he deserved his good fortune, for he was the most honest, pious, and reasonable boy that one could find anywhere. He soon had occasion to display all these virtues under very dramatic circumstances, and they helped to get him out of a very tight corner indeed.

Putiphar's wife was not worthy of the upright man she had married. She was both wicked and deceitful and, having at first lost her head about Joseph and been gently reproved by him, she took a bitter dislike to him. To injure him, she reported to her husband that the young Israelite had shown her grave disrespect. Putiphar hesitated to believe that his well-beloved servant had behaved badly, but his wife insisted so much in her demand for a severe punishment, and produced so many apparent proofs of the slave's wrongdoing, that Putiphar gave way to her and had Joseph cast into prison.

Even after he had exchanged the comforts of Putiphar's palace for the gloom of a prison cell, Joseph did not allow himself to fall into despair. In prison he showed himself so good and brave that the chief keeper himself became his friend. In the depths of his misfortune he continued to pray to God and to implore His aid. And God, who had planned a great destiny for this remarkable youth, continued to protect him.

When Joseph went to prison he found there two very important people, both of them in the service of Pharao. We are not told the exact nature of the charge against them, but it probably was the misuse of public money. The two prisoners were anxiously waiting for the king to pass judgment on them. One morning each of them told of a strange dream he had had during the night. Neither of them knew the meaning of his dream, but Joseph, among his many other talents, possessed that of interpreting dreams.

"Your dream," he told one of the men, "means that Pharao will be merciful to you and will restore you to your former place. As for you," he told the second, "your dream brings you the worst of tidings. The king will have you hanged, and the birds of the air shall devour your body on the gibbet."

Things turned out exactly as Joseph had predicted, and his fame spread far and wide. Soon all Egypt was talking about the little Hebrew prisoner who was such a wonderful interpreter of dreams. . . .

Now it so happened that just at this moment, Pharao himself, the all-powerful king, was greatly troubled by a dream. In this dream he found himself on the banks of the Nile watching seven beautiful cattle, glossy-coated and fat, as they grazed in a marshy pasture. Suddenly, seven other lean and hideously ugly cattle rushed out from the swamp, fell on the fat cattle and devoured them. (To be quite truthful, this was an absurd dream, for who ever saw a cow eat meat? But we all know how senseless and ridiculous things happen in dreams.)

When the king awoke, he asked his priests and soothsayers for the meaning of his dream, but no one would undertake the task, for the odds were that it meant something evil. Someone at the court then thought of the young Israelite prisoner. Pharao sent for him at once, ordering that he be given a bath and provided with fine clothing. How handsome and intelligent Joseph looked when he appeared before the king!

"Sire," Joseph told him, "your dream is easy to understand. The seven fat cattle mean that in your kingdom there will be seven years of rich and abundant harvests. But these years will be followed by seven years of complete drought—the seven lean cattle—and during this period of scarcity your subjects will use up all their reserves of food and there will be risk of famine."

Hearing this, the king threw up his hands to heaven and cried, "But what do you think should be done in order to escape this terrible threat?"

"It is really quite simple," Joseph said modestly but firmly. "Make me your governor over the land of Egypt, responsible for everything, and I will see to it that your people do not die of hunger."

The king then took a gold ring from his finger and a jeweled chain from around his neck and gave them to the young Israelite. And that is how Joseph came to govern the country of the Nile.

Here we must interrupt this romantic story to ask ourselves one question. Is it true history, or is it just a story? Perhaps you have already learned something in school about Egyptian civilization: the pyramids, the Sphinx, the obelisks, and the embalming of mummies. We know so much about ancient Egypt that we have the right to ask if there is anything in Egyptian history to confirm the Bible story of Joseph.

There most certainly is. First of all, it has been possible to reckon that Joseph's sojourn in Egypt took place some 1600 years before the Christian era, and we know that at that time the land was under the rule of kings who had come from Asia and had won it by force of arms. The Hebrews were also Asiatics, which explains why the Pharao should have felt himself in sympathy with Joseph.

In the matter of dreams, we know that the Egyptians attached great importance to them and always sought their meaning. Pharao's dream is easily understood by anyone who knows Egypt. As we have already noted, the country would be a desert were it not for the waters of the Nile. This is the river that overflows its valley each year, irrigating and fertilizing the land so that it bears rich crops. If, however, it should happen in one or several years that the waters of the river did not rise sufficiently for it to overflow its banks, then—because it never rains in the Nile valley—would come drought and famine, the lean years following the fat ones.

And here is further proof that this whole story is completely true: among the many paintings that adorn the tombs of ancient Egypt, there are several of the king's chief ministers, and these all depict the gold ring and the heavy neck chain, worn exactly as the Bible tells us Joseph wore them. On this point, as on so many others, the evidence of history affirms the truth of the Bible story.

It was now Joseph's duty to govern the land of Egypt and to see to it that the Egyptian people be spared famine when the period of the lean years arrived. Right well did he do his work. During the rich years he gave orders to lay by huge quantities of wheat and all kinds of other food, forbidding waste and imposing on the people what we would call a rationing system. So, when the period of scarcity came, he was easily able to feed all the people from his overflowing granaries, and this at a time when neighboring nations were in the grip of famine and were flocking to the banks of the Nile to beg for a little wheat.

It was a great triumph for Joseph, who now was rich and ranked high in the land. He had married a girl of the Egyptian nobility and had several fine children. Finally, God gave him the opportunity of revenging himself on his brothers, and we are going to hear how he availed himself of it.

During the seven years of famine the Israelite tribes, like so many others, came to Egypt in search of food. One day a group of Hebrews who had come to beg for bread were brought before the governor. In a flash, Joseph recognized them as his brothers. In spite of the years that had passed, he was not mistaken: they really were his brothers. All powerful as he was, now was his chance to avenge their past cruelty to him. But such a thought never entered his mind. He questioned them for a time without revealing himself to them. He asked them who they were and from where had they come. They came from Asia, did they? That was suspicious! Were they spies sent by Egypt's enemies? Trembling, the famishing Hebrews protested their innocence.

But Joseph could no longer restrain his emotion. He looked at Benjamin, the youngest of his brothers, and thought how much he resembled their mother. "Do you not know me?" he cried. "I am your brother Joseph." When they bowed down before him in terror and remorse (see how that old dream about the sheaves had been fulfilled), he raised them up and embraced each of them affectionately. "I forgive you with all my heart," he told them. "Go back with all haste to the land of Chanaan, to our aged father, and tell him that I am the most respectful and loving of sons. Bring him back here with you, and I will give you land in Egypt so that you can settle here and never again run the risk of famine."

As Joseph said, so was it done. He who believes in God should forgive injuries done to him as Joseph forgave his brothers. And that is how the children of Israel first settled in Egypt (see map on back endpaper), in a district called Gessen, not far from the Nile delta.

VII

Moses Sets His People Free

"O LORD, OUR GOD, have pity on us! O Lord, our Protector, protect us from our persecutors. God, who of old promised us Your friendship, save us, for we shall perish!"

All day long these plaints echoed throughout the land of Gessen where lived Jacob's descendants. Three centuries had passed since Joseph had established his brothers there, and during those three hundred years nothing very noteworthy seems to have happened to the Israelites. There is a proverb which says, "Happy is the nation that has no history," and we may therefore assume that the Israelites were happy during this period, reaping rich harvests from the good Egyptian soil, watching their flocks increase, and growing rich on trade with the townspeople. One thing we do know, and that is that they remained absolutely loyal to the worship of the True God and would have nothing to do with the ox-headed or eagle-headed idols adored by the Egyptians. But now this pleasant existence had been suddenly brought to an end. A terrible persecution broke out against them, and it was because of this that night and day these poor people uttered their complaints in tears and lamentations.

What had happened to bring this persecution on their heads? Perhaps the Egyptians had become anxious at seeing these foreigners grow in numbers and power. Or perhaps they envied the Israelites their great wealth. Men's actions are often determined by sordid envy. But it is possible that there were also other reasons for the persecution.

During the three centuries that the people of Israel had lived in Egypt, a sort of revolution, or rather a national uprising, had taken place in the land of the Nile. The Asiatic kings who, as we have seen, ruled the country in Joseph's time, had been overthrown and driven out. The true national dynasty of Pharaos had regained the throne. It is easy to understand that once they had freed themselves of the foreign usurpers, the Egyptians loathed anything that reminded them of foreign tyranny. The Hebrews too were Asiatics and were even spoken of as the "Asian plague." It was easy to work off old hatreds on them.

It must be said that the new Pharaos showed themselves to be remarkably able rulers of the country. They were victorious in various wars along their frontiers and added several important provinces to their territory in the north. They built splendid monuments whose ruins can still be seen. One of these Pharaos, Rameses II, who ruled from B.C. 1290 to B.C. 1225, was a very great king and he is well remembered to this day. His mummified body has been found, and is to be seen in the Museum of Cairo; his great temples of Luxor and Karnak give proof of the glory of his reign, and one of the obelisks which adorned them was presented to France by Egypt a hundred years ago. It stands in the middle of the Place de la Concorde in Paris and is a familiar sight to all who visit that city.

It was this line of Egyptian Pharaos, and particularly Rameses II, who persecuted the Hebrews so cruelly. Thousands and thousands of laborers were needed to complete the gigantic structures that he was having built. It was very convenient to recruit them by force from people who did not have to be paid for their labor. Then, when the Israelites protested, in order to terrify them the Egyptians oppressed them even more sorely, even going to the length of ordering the killing at birth of all the little Israelite boys. That is why God's chosen people cried their distress to Heaven, and why the Lord God, Who had promised them protection, heard their prayer and intervened to save them.

I have already told you a little in the first chapter of this book of the beautiful and wonderful story of Moses, who freed his people from the oppression of the Egyptians. Now listen to the charming and touching story of how his life commenced.

The mothers were filled with despair when the Egyptian kings gave the order to kill all newborn Hebrew boys. But one of these mothers had found a clever way of saving the life of her little son. She kept watch upon that part of the river bank where the king's daughter came to bathe. She built a tiny boat of bulrushes coated with tar, which just fitted her baby. When the princess came to bathe, the mother placed her baby adrift in this floating cradle, so that the current of the river would carry it down to the bather. The Pharao's daughter, moved to pity at sight of the abandoned child, rescued it and brought it back to her father's palace. She named the baby Moses, which meant, "saved from the waters."

As he grew up, Moses never forgot that he was one of the unhappy and persecuted people of Israel to whom long ago God had promised such great things. His mother (she must have been most resourceful) had succeeded in persuading the princess to employ her as her son's nurse, and she never ceased to tell him the glorious history of the descendants of Abraham and to instruct him in the true religion of God.

Moses had grown into a handsome and sturdy young man when one day, having gone for a walk past a building-yard, he saw a scene that revolted him. An Egyptian overseer was beating a defenseless Hebrew so cruelly that the unhappy man had collapsed under the rains of blows. Moses was seized by a righteous anger and, turning on the cruel Egyptian, he killed him.

After this, of course, he had to flee, or he would have most certainly been arrested by the Egyptian police. He, therefore, took refuge in the almost deserted mountains on the frontiers of Asia, where he lived as a shepherd. All this time the people of Israel groaned under Egyptian oppression and prayed to God in long lamentations.

One day Moses was alone with his herds on a wild mountain

called Horeb. Suddenly a great flame of fire burst forth before his eyes. This flame seemed to come from a bush, one of those thorny clumps so common in that country, but the astonishing thing about this flame was that though it burned straight from the bush, the latter did not catch fire. Amazed and uneasy, Moses finally understood that this was no natural fire. What could it be? Was it the shining radiance of an angel, or perhaps still more wonderful, of God Himself?

The Voice of the Lord God resounded in his ears.

"Moses! Moses!"

Trembling and stammering in fear, Moses replied, "Lord, here I am. What would You have me do?"

"I have seen the sufferings of the people of Israel and I have heard their cry. Long, long ago, I gave My promise to Abraham, your ancestor, that I would protect his descendants. So I am going to save the Hebrew people from the persecutions of the Egyptians. And it is you, Moses, on whom I am imposing this mission. You will lead your brethren out of Egypt!"

"Lord," replied Moses who had fallen face down upon the ground, "I am but a poor man without the gifts of words or the strength needed for such a task. I am not the man for it. . . ."

But God bade Moses to be silent. To give him some idea of His powers, He said to His faithful servant, "Look at the rod that you carry in your hand." At once the rod turned into a serpent and then back into a rod again. "Hold out your hand itself!" Moses did so, and the skin of the hand became covered with the horrible incurable sores of the leper, only to become clean and healthy in the next moment. God promised Moses that He would give him the power to perform such miracles himself.

Finally, God told Moses something of even greater importance which had never before been revealed to anyone:

"Hear My words, My faithful servant. Until now no one among your people has known My true Name. I am called the Lord God, the Most High, or the All Powerful. But I have a Name just as a man has, since I am a living Being, and that Name should only be pronounced kneeling in fear and trembling. That Name is Yahweh. It is to you I reveal this. Each time that you call to Me by My Name, I will come instantly to your aid, and your enemies will be powerless against you."

The names of the idols of the pagan people were jealously guarded secrets. In revealing His Name to Moses, God pledged Himself to the service of his people, permitting Moses to call on Him at all times. The word Yahweh means "He Who Is," that is, "He alone who exists." He was indeed the One True God.

Convinced by these promises and marks of favor, Moses accepted the task laid on him by God.

It was after this that Moses, as we have already seen, compelled Pharao to allow the Hebrews to depart. The king did not at all relish the idea of parting with such a large unpaid labor force. Where could he find people to replace all those masons and bricklayers? God had to intervene in order to force him to make up his mind.

When the plagues descended on Egypt, Pharao thought at first that they were due to natural causes. Flies and other insects are not rare in Eastern countries; the waters of the Nile had become polluted before; having the crops ruined by hail was nothing new. As for the locusts that came in vast swarms like clouds to strip the fields of every atom of vegetation, they are such a common calamity in Egypt that even to this day a series of security measures are in force to combat them. But, when misfortune followed misfortune, when livestock died, when men's flesh was covered with abscesses and ulcers, and when a terrible darkness spread over the entire country, the heart of Pharao became filled with terror.

As each new plague struck, as each new wound opened in the heart of Egypt, Moses told Pharao unceasingly, "Let us go, and God's anger will be appeased!"

When, however, God saw that the persecutors of Israel remained stubborn in their evil determination, He decided to smite them with a still more terrible affliction. This was the tenth plague which brought misery to every family in the land of the Nile.

God warned Moses so that he could tell the king what was about to happen. At midnight, the Angel of the Lord would pass over the entire kingdom. He would enter every house. And everywhere he would slay all first-born living things: the first-born children, the first-born lambs, the first-born horses. . . . It would be a dreadful massacre, a woe and ruin so terrible that it could hardly be imagined.

If this method did not compel Pharao to yield, it is hard to think of any other that would. It was necessary, however, to make sure that the Angel of Death should make no mistake and that none of the Hebrew households should be harmed.

"As for your people," commanded the Lord God, "let each family sacrifice a lamb. With its blood write a sign on the door of every house, so that my dread messenger will not enter. During the night when this supreme scourge falls on Egypt, you will make ready for your departure. You will remain up, dressed for traveling, and you will eat the lamb you sacrifice, cooked simply on a spit, with unleavened bread, in order to show clearly that you are about to take your departure. Thus there can be no mistake, and none of your people will be harmed by the Angel."

Everything came to pass as God had said. The Hebrews marked the doors of their houses with blood, and ate the lamb with unleavened bread. The Angel of Death passed them by. . . . And it is in memory of the events of this mysterious night that, generation after generation, the chosen people have celebrated the Passover, which means "the passage." We Christians remember it too when we celebrate the Sacrifice of Our Lord Jesus Christ. By His death He saved us, just as the humble lamb saved the Israelites, and He is often called "the Lamb of God."

Now let us turn our eyes to the escaping Hebrews, fleeing in ragged columns from Egypt in the gray light of dawn. It must have been a sorry sight, this Exodus! The people had loaded on to donkeys, camels and carts all their baggage and provisions, the old people and the young children, perhaps a few sticks of furniture. All the time they were looking back fearfully for the first sign of Pharao's cavalry, his chariots with archers to shoot them down.

It was only after they had crossed the Red Sea dry shod, thanks to the miracle for which Moses had called on God, and had seen the pursuing army perish beneath the waves, that once more they were able to breathe easily.

They now commenced their journey across a desert that became more and more forbidding as they advanced. But, what did that matter? They were free at last, and in that great pillar of cloud by day and of fire by night that ever moved in front of their column, they recognized the guidance of God and knew that they were under His protection.

VIII

The Story of Moses Continued: The Ten Commandments

HAVE YOU EVER TRIED to picture for yourself what a desert really is? Life is not easy in such lands. Vast expanses of sand and gravel with, here and there, an occasional bush, gray and shriveled. During the day the merciless sun beats down from a sky of monotonous blue, while at night the cold is so intense that the traveler shivers even under a heavy woolen cloak. Sandstorms frequently sweep across these great plains, irritating skin, mouth, eyes, and hands with millions of what feel like pin pricks. If it rains, which happens once every two or three years, the rains come with the force of a cloudburst and threaten the traveler with drowning.

You can understand, therefore, how uncomfortable and perilous was the flight of the Hebrews across the desert. It was a problem to supply even the bare human needs of food and drink. Water was scarce and such few wells as lay in the travelers' path all too often contained only filthy and foul-tasting water. And where in this desert was food to be found for the thousands upon thousands of fugitives who had left Egypt? The supplies they brought with them were running out quickly. Along the way they could find no food.

Even among the Hebrews there were grumblers who never stopped saying, "Why has this Moses made us leave Egypt? To die like animals in the desert? Has all our trouble been for this? By the banks of the Nile we at least had enough to eat. Do you remember the lovely fresh fruit we had in Egypt, the tasty meat dishes, and those wonderful onions?" So the brainless few that are to be found among people everywhere babbled to their fellow voyagers. Had they already forgotten their miserable existence in the country of the Nile, and the persecution they had suffered?

Moses, aided by his brother Aaron, and helped unceasingly by the All Powerful God, kept firm control over the mass of his followers. To feed and shelter his people, Moses only needed to use the miraculous powers which God had given to him.

On one occasion, in response to the prayer of Moses, who feared that his people would be reduced to starvation, a great flock of quail, no doubt migrating from Africa to Europe, alighted near the Israelite camp. We can imagine the feasting that took place that night! On another occasion, when all reserves of food had been consumed, Moses, sleepless from care, spent the entire night praying to God for help. When morning came, the Israelites found scattered on the ground a strange substance which seemed to have fallen from the skies. It proved to be not merely edible but delicious, a nutty-flavored mixture of gum that appeared in small balls. It was manna, sent by God to feed His people. From then on, this mysterious food was to continue to appear for as long as the Hebrews were in the desert lands.

It was the same thing in the matter of drinking water. One day when the people were tortured with thirst, God told Moses to strike with his rod a rock that seemed completely dry; and, as soon as he did so, a clear stream of water burst forth from it, enough to slake the thirst not merely of the travelers but of their animals as well. God always makes response to those who trust in Him!

The direct route from Egypt to the land of Chanaan would have been northward along the sea coast (see map on back endpaper). It was not possible for the Hebrews to follow this road because it led through country occupied by warlike tribes. They were called Philistines, and we shall soon hear more about them. The Hebrews had therefore to make an immense detour in the form of a triangle around the peninsula of Sinai which juts out into the Red Sea.

Even this road was not particularly safe. It was infested with hostile and plundering Bedouins, and several times the Israelites had to fight them off. A serious pitched battle took place at Raphidim, but here again God was true to His word and saved His children. Moses established himself on the summit of a hill from which he could watch the struggle on the plain below him. When he saw his men recoiling, he raised his arms toward God, and at once the enemy fell back. As long as Moses prayed, Israel had the upper hand, but the moment he lowered his arms or prayed less fervently, the Bedouins advanced. Finally, victory went to the chosen people, who were able to resume their search.

They finally reached the foot of Mount Sinai. This is a bleak and strange mountain, its slopes littered with a wild confusion of great rocks. All round is a gloomy outcrop of black and red volcanic lava. The vertical cliff sides are cut by dark gorges where no waters flow, and the peak, 8500 feet high, is often obscured by storm clouds and shaken by peals of thunder which echo and re-echo incessantly from the faces of the cliffs.

In these terrifying surroundings, the people of Israel were overcome by fear. The smoke and flames from the crater of the volcano terrified them, and surely this terrible thunder was the voice of an angry God! There was one among them, Moses, who was not afraid, for he knew the meaning of these manifestations of nature. The sound of a mysterious trumpet called to him from the clouds that enveloped the summit of the mountain. Inspired by God, the great leader of his people recognized the call and made haste, alone, to scale the peak.

When he arrived there, a dense cloud enveloped him and thunder and lightning played all around him. The earth shook violently and the volcano belched forth smoke as from a furnace. In the midst of these terrors a great Voice resounded, and Moses recognized it. It was the same Voice that long ago, and almost in the same place, had spoken to him from the burning bush; it was the Voice of God. Bowed down upon the earth, Moses awaited the commands of the Lord.

"Moses, My faithful servant, you know My power. You have seen how I have dealt with the Egyptians and how I have protected you and your people in your journey here. I have done this because of the old alliance established long ago between Me and your father, Abraham. Guard and cherish this covenant and obey Me at all times. It is My will that you shall be a holy nation, the people who shall be My witness upon the earth.

"And now, listen to My Words! Take two tablets of stone and write on them what I am about to tell you: these are My Commandments, the ten laws that all men on earth must obey under pain of My punishment. You will teach them to the people of Israel, My people, so that they shall be the first to conform to them."

You know these Ten Commandments very well, of course. They are the "Commandments of God," which you learned in your catechism. How simple and beautiful they are! To adore the True God, to honor our parents, not to steal or kill, or tell lies or to injure anyone. If only all men lived up to these principles how much better would things go in the world than they do now!

The Voice became silent, the dark cloud that had hidden the mountain tops moved away. Moses stood up. He was alone. The Tablets of the Law of God, the Decalogue, lay beside him. He took them upon his shoulder and came down into the plains. Had we seen him at that moment, we would have understood at once that this man had been through a great experience, for his face was radiant; one would have said that a supernatural brightness came forth from him, a reflection of the Light of God.

But when Moses came down from the mountain and reached the tents of his people, what an abominable sight greeted his eyes! In the very middle of the camp had been set up one of those animal-headed statues such as were to be seen in Egypt. How magnificently it shone in the firelight, this abominable Golden Calf! And the Israelites were bowing and singing and dancing and making merry all around this hideous image.

How on earth had such a thing come to happen? While Moses was away, some discontented Israelites had complained of him to their companions, saying, "Now see what he has done, this fine Moses of yours! He has led us here under the pretense that it was God's command that we should leave Egypt. Here we are in this horrible desert, with nothing to eat but manna and we are sick of the taste of it. Now Moses has abandoned us! He tells us that he has gone up to the mountain, but the truth of the matter is that he is afraid to face us and has run away. Let us, therefore, follow the example of the Egyptians and worship a real divinity whose image we can make for ourselves, not this invisible God that Moses is always talking about! We will set up a Golden Calf; you will see it is he who will get us out of our troubles." It is sad to have to relate that the people listened willingly to the advice of these wicked counselors.

The anger of Moses when he saw what had been done was terrifying. This faithless people, he said, was unworthy to receive the Commandments of the Most High! Forthwith he hurled the Tablets of the Law to the ground, breaking them into pieces. Then he stormed through the camp, loudly reproaching his people and reminding them of all the favors they had received from God, so that they would understand the full horror of their treachery toward Him.

Some of the Israelites were stricken with remorse. Rallying around Moses, they attacked those who had set up the Golden Calf. The people came to their senses. The Calf was thrown from its pedestal and broken into fragments, and the ringleaders in the revolt were slain.

When things settled down after this crisis, Moses was able to explain to the Israelites all that God had told him. He taught them the Ten Commandments and ordered that from now on these were to be the law for the whole nation. As God had commanded, one day of the week was to be devoted entirely to prayer: this was the Sabbath Day, which Israel observed as a day of complete rest. From the Sabbath comes our Sunday, the day when work is forbidden and when we should especially pray to God.

A great chest, made of precious wood and covered in pure gold was now built in order to hold the Tablets of the Law. At each corner there was a gold rung through which poles could be slipped so that the chest could be easily carried. On the lid of the chest the statues of two angels, the cherubim, spread their wings over it as though to protect its contents. So was made the Ark of the Covenant, a small portable temple, very suitable to the needs of a nomadic people. One complete tribe, the Levites, were entrusted with the service of the Ark. It was their duty to guard and carry it and to organize public prayers, and because of this the Levites became the priests of Israel.

The people now resumed their march, and once more the long columns wound along the desert tracks. Once more they were assailed by hunger and thirst, and once more they had to depend on manna and on water miraculously brought forth by Moses with his rod. And again there were complaints, protests, and revolts against Moses; for people shrink from hardship and difficulty even when these are endured in a great cause. But Moses was unflinching in his purpose. He would bring his people to the Promised Land, that Land of Chanaan which had been the country of their ancestors and which, long ago, God had promised to Abraham for his descendants.

When their journey was nearing its end, the people halted to rest and refresh themselves at the oasis of Cades (see map on back endpaper), where they took shelter for a long time. During this sojourn Moses completed the organization of the nation of Israel, so that it would be better able to overcome the enemies it was sure to meet, and to properly govern the country of Chanaan from the moment they occupied it. The existing division of the people into twelve tribes, each called after one of Jacob's sons, formed the basis of the new state. This tribal organization remained the same throughout the centuries that were to come.

Chanaan—the Promised Land! With what longing and affection the Israelites had dreamed of it, during their long wanderings in the desert. Many years had passed since the exodus from Egypt, and those who were old at the time were long since dead; those who had been children were now grown up. But hope burned bright in the hearts of all, hope for this holy land where man could spend his life happily in the service of God.

From Cades, Moses sent messengers into Chanaan to spy out the land and to report back to him. When they returned they brought back magnificent fruit with them: figs, pomegranates, and a bunch of grapes so heavy that it took two men to carry it. They also, however, brought back news of a less pleasing kind. The country was populated by a warlike, strong, and well-armed people whose towns were not likely to yield easily. "No matter!" cried the Israelites. If there had to be fighting they would fight. But, come what might, the land promised by God to Israel was going to be Israelite!

This was the last order given by Moses. He made his people advance east of the Dead Sea, so as to attack the country on the flank where the defenses were likely to be weak. The great leader had grown old, very old. He was now one hundred and twenty years of age. He wondered if he was to die before he entered the Promised Land. Was this supreme joy to be denied him?

God had decided that it was. Even the greatest saints can commit sins, and Moses had been guilty of one. One day in the desert when God had ordered him to strike the rock with his rod in order to bring forth water, there had been a moment of disobedience. It surely was not possible that this dusty and barren rock could yield water! He struck it only reluctantly and with hesitation. He, the man of supreme faith, had doubted God. It was in punishment for this sin that God ordained that he should die before he entered the Promised Land.

To the east of Chanaan, there is a steep mountain called Mount Nebo which rises to nearly four thousand feet and overlooks the Valley of the Jordan River (see map on front endpaper). From its summit there is a fine view of the red hills and tree-bordered rivers of Palestine.

For a long time, Moses gazed from afar on the Promised Land. Then he died (probably about the year 1180 B.C). As his tomb was never discovered, Israelite tradition has it that God came to seek the body of His faithful servant and carried it to heaven.

IX

How Josue Entered the Land of Chanaan

NOW, BEFORE WE FOLLOW the Hebrews in their entry into Chanaan, let us try to form a true picture of this country where the events of twelve hundred years of history are about to take place.

When we think of the Holy Land or Palestine (those are, you know, other names for Chanaan), we are inclined to think of a fairly large country; so many things happened there, so many famous people lived in it. But this is not so. The territory of Chanaan is very small, less than ten thousand square miles. The distance from the northern to the southern boundary is barely one hundred and fifty miles—an easy three hours run in an automobile. An airplane could cross the country from east to west in fifteen minutes.

Although it is so small, the different regions of this little country vary greatly. Let us then journey through it from north to south and see what we shall find on the way (of course we should look at the map in the front endpaper of this book). Right on the northern frontier is an impressive mountain, over eight thousand feet high, which in spring is clad in snow. This is Mount Hermon, called in the Bible "the eldest among mountains," whose proud reflection is mirrored in the clear waters of the Lake of Tiberias. South of this we come to a land of gently rolling hills; this is the smiling and fertile land of Galilee, dotted with white villages surrounded by cypress groves. Further south still in Samaria, fold after fold of mountains separated from each other by plains. Then comes Judea, a rugged and tangled mass of reddish-colored hills which finally becomes empty of human habitation and animal life. Here we meet the desert.

Let us now travel east from the coast, where the lovely Mediterranean Sea washes the shores of Palestine, and see what we find there. First of all the rich plains and valleys, such as Saron, filled with olive plantations and orchards. Then, little by little, the land rises until we seem to be on a mountain plateau, although in fact we are only about 1900 to 2000 feet above sea level. The highest mountains are Mount Thabor (1850 feet), Mount Garizim (2800 feet), and Mount Djermag (3700 feet). It is that strange natural phenomenon known as the Valley of the Jordan that gives us the impression of being much higher up than we really are.

The River Jordan—how many times its name crops up in the history of Israel! If you look at the map at the beginning of this book you will be able to follow its course clearly. It rises in the wooded slopes of Mount Hermon and flows due south until it empties itself into the Dead Sea. The Jordan valley is an immense canyon, a deep wound in the surface of the earth, no doubt caused by a great earthquake. And as there is no passage between it and the Mediterranean Sea, the waters of the latter are unable to reach it; also it is far below sea level. The surface of the lakes of Tiberias or Genesareth are six hundred feet below that of the coast. It is not hard to imagine the summer heat of this stifling corridor, above all in the neighborhood of the Dead Sea where the heavily salted waters lie motionless beneath a brazen sky. In the springtime, however, the Jordan valley enjoys a perfect climate.

Despite its small size, Chanaan is a picturesque and varied land. Let us now consider the richness of its products.

In the Bible, the Hebrews describe the Promised Land as a region of astonishing fertility, a second Garden of Eden, a land "overflowing with milk and honey." This description is perhaps a bit exaggerated, but it is not surprising when we remember that it was given by people fresh from their long wanderings in the desert. It is no wonder that they were lost in admiration of the green fields, the orchards and the palm groves of Chanaan.

And it is quite true that Palestine is a very lovely country. The sky overhead is a deep blue, the soil is reddish or ocher in color, and cypress trees line the hillsides. The plains are clothed in golden cornfields and olive plantations of silver gray. In the lower parts of the Jordan valley, date palms yield their succulent crop. Everywhere bloom roses, jasmine, and the vine with large purple flowers called bougainvilla. Imagine for yourself great flights of storks passing over the fields, and you will get some idea of the full beauty of the landscape.

Although much of the country is fertile, much of it consists of waterless hills, dusty and barren, gloomy expanses of shriveled vegetation where everything is parched and yellow, including the livestock that tries to exist on such poor feeding. Palestine therefore is by no means entirely fertile, but it has many rich districts where men and livestock can keep themselves in comfort. When the Hebrews occupied Palestine they had the choice of earning a living either by grazing their flocks on the hillside and open plains, or by cultivating crops in the well-watered valleys.

They found a third occupation for themselves in commerce. If you look at the map in the front of this book, you will see for yourself that Chanaan was a natural trade route. The traveler from Asia Minor to Egypt had to cross Palestine from north to south, while the caravans from Babylon to the Mediterranean coast had also to traverse it. The seaports of Chanaan are not very good because the coast is level and sandy; there is only one natural harbor, the bay protected by the slopes of Mount Carmel. The land trade routes, on the other hand, were of great importance; and we shall see how, throughout the long centuries of Israel's history, there ceaselessly passed to and fro great caravans of camels, mules, and donkeys laden with all the produce of the East.

Such then, was the country which God had promised to His chosen people. This was the land at which, from the summits of the mountains overlooking the Dead Sea, the Hebrews gazed with such longing. The difficulty was that, in order to settle in the country, they must first take possession of it, and this promised to be no easy task.

Who were the actual owners of Chanaan when the Hebrews were about to invade it? Here we find a rather confused state of affairs.

During the preceding centuries Chanaan, the high road between Asia and Africa, had belonged sometimes to the Pharaos of Egypt and sometimes to the kings of Mesopotamia. Frequent battles between these two powers had been fought on its soil. At the period of which we are writing, that is, about the year 1180 B.C., it belonged to neither, for both these great powers had their hands full in defending themselves against formidable invaders.

The Aryans were attacking all the Mediterranean lands. You will remember that these Aryans were our ancestors, from whom are descended the Greeks, Romans, Gauls, and most of the other European peoples. They made their appearance about the twelfth century B.C., and were much better armed than their opponents. They had mounted troops, and their weapons were of iron and steel, whereas at this time both the Egyptians and the Mesopotamians only knew how to forge weapons of bronze.

These Aryan invasions brought about wars in all the Mediterranean lands. There is one of which you have no doubt heard: this was the Trojan war, the story of which has been told by the great Greek poet Homer. The siege of Troy and the adventures of Agamemnon and Ulysses took place exactly at the time when the Hebrews made their attack on Chanaan.

The Aryan invasions gave the people of Israel their opportunity. While the Egyptian Pharao and the king of Babylon were far too busy repelling attacks on their own territories to have time to worry about what was happening in the small country of Chanaan, the Hebrews had their chance of occupying it.

This does not mean that they had not enemies, and plenty of them, to fight. The towns were occupied by Chanaanites, the descendants of those we saw there in the days of the Patriarchs. Over the plains and deserts roamed dangerous tribes of Bedouins, the Amalecites and the Edomites, who dwelled in tents and divided their time between herding their flocks and preying on passing caravans. Finally, the richest part of the country, the coastal area in the south, had been occupied by a force of Aryans who had been driven out of Egypt. They were called the Philistines, and they gave the name Palestine to the territory they had seized. So you can see that the Hebrews had no easy task before them if they were to defeat all these adversaries.

Fortunately for them, Moses had chosen as his successor a fine leader, Josue, who had been his assistant during the long journey in the desert. God Himself had promised that He would aid the new Israelite leader, and ordered him to launch his attack on Chanaan.

Josue's first difficulty was to get his people across the River Jordan. At the point of crossing, the river was no less than two hundred and fifty feet wide, and in flood. Josue, however, had absolute confidence in God; surely the All Powerful, who had brought His people dryshod across the Red Sea, would not fail to help them across the river. He ordered the Levites carrying the Ark of the Covenant to march straight into the current. Lo! as they did so, the waters stopped as though their passage were barred by an iron wall, and so the entire column crossed in safety to the opposite bank. Here they halted for a while in order to make preparations for the attack, to erect a monument of thanksgiving to God, and to celebrate the feast of the Passover which had been instituted by Moses in Egypt.

Some twenty or thirty miles from the Israelite camp, perched on its steep hill, stood the proud town of Jericho, one of the strong citadels of the Chanaanites. Situated in the hot climate of the Lower Jordan, the city was, due to its abundant springs of water, the center of a wonderfully fertile oasis. It was renowned for its date palms, its roses, and its honey, and its citizens took no small pride in their abundant wealth. Sheltered by their strong walls, they gazed down scornfully at this horde of wandering tribesmen who had the audacity to threaten them.

Josue, however, did not hesitate. He began the siege, probably using the Assyrian method of undermining the walls by driving long tunnels under them. This would have been a tedious and lengthy operation, so once more the Lord God came to the assistance of His faithful people. On the order of Josue, the priests carrying the Ark of the Covenant began to march in procession seven times around the city walls, blowing their trumpets as they marched. This caused great amusement to the people of Jericho. They laughed at the absurd Hebrews for imagining they could cause their walls to collapse by blowing trumpets at them. But suddenly, at the exact moment when the seventh circuit of the walls had been completed, an ominous noise was heard. Just as though they really had been undermined by tunnels, the mighty ramparts of Jericho tum-

bled down in ruins. Rushing in to the assault, the Israelites captured the town which had been laid open to them by a miracle of God.

From now on, the chosen people had a foothold in the Promised Land. Seeing what had happened, the Chanaanites united to defend themselves, and the people of five cities joined forces to repel the attackers. Josue's military skill was too great for them. Taking them by surprise, he inflicted a crushing defeat upon them, the memory of which is enshrined in Israelite tradition. Shortly after this great battle, an Israelite poet composed a song to celebrate the glorious victory, and in this song he tells us that, at the height of the battle Josue cried out, "Move not, O sun, toward the mountains nor thou, O moon, toward the valley. And the sun and the moon stood still, till the people revenged themselves of their enemies."

Victories such as this—and there were many others—brought the Israelites deep into the land of Chanaan. Josue had divided the country into twelve parts, allotting one to each tribe; and each tribe had to conquer its own territory for itself. When Josue died at the age of one hundred and ten, the Israelites were far from possessing all of Palestine, but they were now sufficiently well established to carry on everywhere a struggle that in the course of the next two centuries would make them masters of the land.

X

Israel's "Middle Ages": Battles and Adventures in the Time of the Judges

IT WAS BY AUDACITY, strategy, surprise, and hard fighting that the chosen people established themselves in Chanaan. The struggle cost them dear in blood and tears, and it lasted for two hundred years. We will now read of some of the picturesque adventures that took place during this period.

We must understand of course that, when the Hebrews forced their way in, the original inhabitants of the country were not at all willing to yield meekly to them. The Chanaanites, Edomites, Amalecites, and Philistines were all hardy warriors, who refused either to submit or to leave. And the Israelites were still far from numerous. Each of the tribes formed only a small core in the territory assigned to it by Josue, and had to fight hard in order to maintain itself and grow in strength.

These two centuries of Hebrew history correspond to what in European history is called the Middle Ages. Just as in the Middle Ages in Europe there was a ceaseless struggle to maintain law and order, so the tribes of Israel were constantly on the alert, and the sword was never out of their hands. As happened in Europe, there appeared among the chosen people men of fiery zeal for the establishment of the religion of the True God. And, just as happened under the feudal system in the West, where we find kings who were also administrators, judges and military leaders, each tribe of Israel elected a leader to perform all these functions.

In the Bible such leaders are called Judges. Many of them are famous for their deeds of arms; for instance, who does not know the name of Samson? All sorts of people appear in this roll of heroes; not merely great kings and generals but ordinary people and even one woman, Debbora, who was the Hebrew Joan of Arc. As for the wiles and strategems of Samson, they remind us forcibly of the tactics employed in France during the Hundred Years' War.

The tribe to which Josue had allotted the most northerly territory of Chanaan found itself engaged in a ceaseless struggle with the local inhabitants. Through this territory passed the all-important road which linked the towns with the desert caravan routes. Because of this, the Chanaanites made life as difficult as possible for the Israelites. Every time the latter tried to secure a foothold in the valley, an enemy army drove them back into the mountains. And they began to grow discouraged.

This was when Debbora appeared on the scene. She was a most remarkable woman, a "prophetess," that is, one who always spoke in the Name of God. She had no patience with the poor spirit shown by the fighting men of Israel, and asked them angrily if they were content to allow these pagan idolators to remain in possession of their fertile plains.

"We have no arms," they told her.

"Well, go and make arms," was her reply.

"The enemy are very strong," was the next objection.

"Not as strong as we are," cried Debbora, "since the Lord Himself has promised us His help." She talked so long and so persuasively that finally the chief of the tribe listened to her. An armed force was organized and a campaign was decided on.

Taking up positions in the mountains overlooking the valley of Cedron, the Israelites lay in wait and watched the threatening movements of the Chanaanite soldiers on the plain below. But when the moment chosen by God arrived, a terrific downpour of rain descended on the valley. The river burst its banks and flooded the land, engulfing many of the Chanaanite chariots and horses.

The Israelites launched their attack from both front and rear, and God's enemies were completely defeated. The Chanaanite king took refuge in flight, but was overtaken and killed—to his greater shame, by a woman. Standing erect on the mountain top from which she had watched the battle, the inspired Debbora broke into a poem of thanksgiving to God: "So let all Thy enemies perish, O Lord: but let them that love Thee shine as the sun shines in his rising."

When all danger from the Chanaanites had passed, the Israelites had another to face: raids and pillage by the Bedouins of the desert. One of the Judges who distinguished himself in the struggle against these dangerous marauders was Gedeon. While still quite young, he had won fame for himself by destroying an idol that was venerated by some of the peasants of his village, for it must be admitted that even among the chosen people there were unbelievers. There were people who forsook the True God to worship local idols and, in particular, one idol called Baal, who was said to be very powerful and very terrible. Now, one evening Gedeon had destroyed the image of this false god, and the following day he had told his people, "You see that god of yours is powerless. I have smashed his image into pieces, and he has not even been able to punish me."

Having thus brought all his tribe back to the true faith," Gedeon was given command of the army with orders to drive the Bedouin raiders back to the desert. He picked three hundred of the strongest and fleetest warriors. He chose these men in a very curious way. Bringing them to the banks of a stream, he ordered each man to drink from it, and he rejected all who drank from their cupped hands, accepting only those who lapped up the water like an eager dog.

Gedeon set off with his men at dead of night and noiselessly surrounded the enemy camp. Each soldier carried a trumpet and had under his arm a lighted torch concealed in an earthenware pot. When Gedeon gave the word his men broke the pots, brandished the torches, and the three hundred trumpets sounded their loudest.

Panic seized the Bedouins in their tents and the chosen people scored another brilliant victory.

In the story of Jephte we find another episode in the struggle against the desert tribes, this time in the south of Chanaan on the slopes of the high ground that overlooks the Dead Sea. Jephte was an adventurer, a young man whose life so far had little to recommend it; but, when danger threatened, his tribe called on him to lead them against the formidable Bedouins. God, as we know, in choosing His servants follows His own rules and not ours, and, when He enlists a man in His service, He completely transforms him.

So it was that Jephte was elected Judge by his tribe and set about organizing an expedition against the enemy. When he was on the point of marching off to war, he made a promise to God: "Lord, if you will deliver my enemies into my hand, I will sacrifice to you the first person who comes before me on my return." This promise shows us that Jephte was not very well instructed in his religion, for it was not God's Will (remember the story of Abraham and Isaac) that human sacrifice be made to Him. Jephte then set out to war and engaged the enemy in a battle in which, thanks to his skillful leadership, his forces won complete victory.

As he returned, what was the first sight that met his eyes? His own daughter, his only child, who with her playmates came out to meet him, singing and dancing to the music of tambourines. The unhappy victor was in despair, but what could he do? He had made a promise and he must keep it, even if it meant the sacrifice of his daughter! The child herself told him that he must fulfill his vow.

The Bible does not tell us clearly what happened to the girl. Was she really put to death? Many students of the Bible do not believe that she was. They suggest that instead she retired to the desert to spend the rest of her life in prayer and thanksgiving for her father's victory, becoming in fact, what we would call a nun. But we do not know what really happened.

Now we come to the most famous of all the Judges: Samson, whose romantic adventures remind us of those of Hercules, Ulysses, Robin Hood, and other legendary heroes. Samson's story, however, contains, as we will see, not merely adventure, but important lessons for us all.

The great enemies of Samson's tribe were the Philistines. They occupied all the rich plains along the Mediterranean coast and prevented the Hebrews from settling there. The Philistines were a race of fair-haired men, very tall and strong, well armed and so skilled in war that the very sight of their plumed helmets struck terror into the hearts of the Israelites. Samson, however, was not in the least afraid of them, for he was a huge and terrifically strong man. He could lift great weights, break a tree in two with his hands, and kill a lion with one blow of his fist. With all this he believed in God, and was His faithful servant. From the day of his birth his parents had dedicated him to the service of the Most High and, as a token of his fidelity to the Lord God, he was commanded never to cut his hair.

You can picture to yourself this long-haired giant as he kept up his relentless struggle with the Philistines. Many exciting incidents took place, and hardly a day passed that he did not play some damaging trick upon his enemies. On one occasion just when the harvest was ripe, he burned the Philistines' crops by loosing in their cornfields foxes with flaming torches tied to their tails.

On another occasion he was captured by a Philistine force and lead away, heavily bound, to prison. On the way he burst his bonds and, seizing the first weapon that came to his hand, which happened to be the jawbone of an ass, he laid about him so vigorously that he destroyed a full thousand of his Philistine captors. Then, free and sprightly, as he went on his way, he composed a little song of triumph: "With the jawbone of an ass I have destroyed them!"

Then there was the time when he made his way into the Philistine town of Gaza. The citizens hastily closed the gates of the city in the hope of trapping him inside, but Samson just tore down both doors of the principal gate and walked away with the doorposts, bolts and all, roaring with laughter, to throw them away on the top of the highest mountain he could find.

As you can well imagine, the Philistines were enraged at being so constantly outwitted. So they had recourse to a trick in order to trap Samson. For this they made use of a very beautiful woman called Dalila. Ever since the days of our mother Eve, women have been the cause of trouble for men, and Dalila deceived Samson completely. She pretended that she loved him more than any man in the world, and the poor giant took her at her word and finally came to trust her completely. Again and again she asked him the secret of his amazing strength. At first Samson refused to tell her, saying that the secret belonged to God. Finally, however, Dalila nagged at him so much that he told her the truth: "I owe my strength to the protection of the Most High. At birth my parents dedicated me to His service and I am commanded never to cut my hair." The treacherous Dalila at last knew the secret she had been sent to seek. And God's punishment was to fall on Samson for his sin in telling it to her.

During the night, while Samson slept, Dalila cut off his hair and then sent for the Philistines. Having lost his power, Samson was now no stronger than any other man. His enemies captured him, put out his eyes, and kept him captive in order to mock at him. It was a terrible punishment but the poor victim only prayed humbly to God to pardon him for his sin.

In the end, God granted Samson one last triumph, for He always forgives those who are truly sorry for their sins. As Samson's hair grew, his strength came back to him. One day, when the Philistines had brought him to one of their palaces in order to make game of him, the Israelite hero grasped in his arms one of the columns that supported the hall and tore it down. There was a sinister rumbling and the whole building collapsed, burying Samson and his enemies in its ruins.

This period of Israel's history is indeed full of stories of violence and bloodshed. Such happenings always take place in times of conquest, but they were not all that happened. As in the case of the Middle Ages in the West, we find in Israel, side by side with warlike exploits, romantic incidents in which women play appealing roles. You remember the story of Tristan and Isolde and of the Lady of Shalot. Well, the Israelites too, among all their accounts of war, preserve from the days of the Judges the story of a simple and humble girl whose great goodness was rewarded by God.

Her name was Ruth and she had married a young Israelite who had brought her to live with him on the high ground overlooking the Dead Sea, the land of Moab. Soon after her marriage, Ruth's husband died and, as her father-in-law had also died, she was left alone with her mother-in-law, who loved her tenderly. This good woman said to her, "Do not stay here with me, return to

your own country where you will find a new husband and fresh happiness." But Ruth knew that her mother-in-law was old and poor. What would become of her should she be left alone? She decided to stay and look after her.

As they were very poor, Ruth had to earn a living for both of them. This she did by following the harvesters in the barley fields, gathering the stalks of barley that were overlooked by the reapers, as was permitted by the law of Moses.

One day a very rich landowner named Booz noticed the fair young gleaner. Having made inquiries about her he learned her story. He was a widower, and he was moved by her unselfish devotion. One night, while the harvesters were asleep in the open field under the brilliant starlight of the East, Booz sought out Ruth and begged her to marry him. So was Ruth's goodness rewarded and, in relating this charming story, the Hebrews say that Ruth reminds them of the human soul which, if it is pure, simple, and capable of wholehearted devotion, is loved and cherished by God.

XI
King David: Warrior and Poet

THE LAST OF THE JUDGES was Samuel. Like Samson, he had at his birth been dedicated by his parents to the service of God, and his holiness and wisdom caused his tribe to choose him as their leader. Indeed at that time it needed great wisdom and sanctity to be a leader in Israel. As their battles went well for them and their enemies weakened, the people began to forget the Commandments of God and misbehaved themselves in all sorts of ways. Even the priests who guarded the Ark of the Covenant sold for their private profit the meats brought to them by the faithful for sacrifice!

As you can well imagine, these sins were not allowed to go unpunished. The Israelites were put to flight by a surprise attack by the Philistines and, still worse, the Ark of the Covenant, the sacred shrine of the Tablets of the Law, fell into the hands of the attackers.

The situation was saved by Samuel. First of all he brought back his people to full obedience to God, showing himself an example of perfect virtue, and then he organized an expedition against the Philistines. The Ark of the Covenant was recovered, and all was well. But the warning had been a severe one.

It was now that the people began to say to each other, "We shall never be done with our enemies unless we combine all our strength. Instead of having one Judge for each tribe, what we want is one single chief over the twelve tribes. We want a king. Other nations have kings, why not we?" And the people were perfectly right in their demand.

God then spoke to Samuel, "Listen to the people and give them a king. When I tell you who he is to be, you will bless him and anoint him King of Israel."

From now on we shall see how the Israelites developed their state into a kingdom like those that already existed on the Nile and the Euphrates. The period—about the year 1040 B.C.—was favorable to the establishment of such a kingdom in Palestine. If the country had been in the hands of a strong power the Israelites would never have been allowed to unite their forces in such a manner, but at this time both Egypt and Mesopotamia were too much taken up with their own troubles to have time to interfere in Chanaan. The kingdom of Egypt was in complete disorder, torn by wars between rival rulers, while Babylon was going through a period of crises and calamity, suffering from great floods and attacked from without by armed raiders. God had chosen well the hour for the birth of the Kingdom of Israel.

One day when Samuel, now a very old man, was engaged in meditation and prayer, a very tall man who looked like a farmer appeared before him, announcing that his name was Saul. He had come, he said, to ask Samuel's advice on a very small matter, but one that mattered a great deal to him. He had lost his flock of she-asses in the mountains and he could not find them. It was well known, he said, that Samuel had a mysterious gift of seeing all sorts of things both in the present and in the future, so could he not tell him where the missing animals were to be found?

All this talk of missing donkeys was, of course, only God's way of bringing Saul to Samuel's notice. The moment Saul appeared before him the old Judge, although he had never seen the man before, recognized him as the one chosen by God to be king of Israel. Taking a flask of holy oil, he anointed Saul on the forehead, consecrating him in the name of God. He then presented Saul to the twelve tribes who accepted him as their king. And that is how Saul mounted the throne of Israel.

Saul's reign lasted for thirty years, and at the beginning it was marked by great victories. Helped by his sons, he inflicted crushing blows on his enemies. He seemed to be everywhere at once. He chased the Bedouins back to their desert, and the Philistines to their plains. He completely reorganized the Israelite army, and it grew in strength. His reign seemed to be a brilliant success.

But it was these very successes that proved to be Saul's undoing. Forgetting that it was God who had chosen him and had given him his victories, his pride grew beyond all reason. On several occasions he broke the commandments of the Law, refused to carry out his promises, and flouted the authority of God's representative, Samuel, who had to reprove him again and again. Finally, God tired of him. He called the old Judge to Him again and said, "Saul has disobeyed Me, and I will have no more to do with him. From now on he will suffer misfortune after misfortune, and you will consecrate as king another man whom I will choose for you."

Affairs now grew desperate, for Saul's conduct became strange and hard to understand. Was he really crazy? Not always, but he had moments of madness when he committed every kind of violence, trying to kill everyone near him. Nowadays we would say that he had a neurosis. His good fortune in war deserted him; no more victories blessed his arms; he found himself surrounded by enemies.

It was now that there appeared in Israel one of the most appealing figures in Bible history. This was a young boy, a lad of perhaps sixteen years of age, graceful in build and with russet hair. He was a youth of great beauty and high intelligence and from his infancy had shown astonishing gifts. While watching his father's flocks he composed poems which he sang to his own accompaniment on a small harp or zither. These poems were so beautiful that to this very day they are sung in our churches to praise God and in prayer to Him.

Guided by God, Samuel went to the village of Bethlehem, where lived this youth, who was called David. He was the youngest of a family of eight boys. To everyone's surprise, Samuel went up to the last born of the family and anointed him on the forehead with holy oil, declaring the shepherd boy henceforth to be the King of Israel. And God did not delay long in making the young man's fame ring through Israel.

All the time these events were taking place the war with the Philistines had continued. In the Philistine forces was a huge giant called Goliath who each day created havoc in the Israelite camp. He had killed so many people that no one any longer dared to oppose him, until one day David offered to fight him.

Goliath burst into a roar of laughter when he saw the foolhardy

boy who dared to face him. This really *was* funny! To send a child against the mighty Goliath! No need for breastplate or helmet here; a stick or cudgel would soon settle this puny brat. But as the giant advanced boastfully, whiz! a stone flew through the air. While watching his flocks David had often practiced with his sling and had become very skillful in its use. Flung with deadly accuracy, the stone from David's sling struck Goliath full on the forehead and he fell to the ground unconscious. The fight ended with David cutting off Goliath's head.

This great triumph made David famous overnight, and all Israel rang with his fame. King Saul sent for the young hero and was very pleased with his graceful appearance and modest bearing. When he discovered that David was also a poet and a wonderful musician, he asked the boy to stay with him as his page. But alas, his mind was again clouded by a dark fit of madness. His heart became filled with envy. It was unbearable that all Israel should sing the praises of this brat! They raved about his wonderful courage and intelligence, while no one had a good word to say for him, the King. One day, as David was playing the zither in the royal chamber, the jealous Saul hurled a lance at him. The nimble David avoided it, but from now on he could not stay with the king, and he had to take refuge in the desert.

Saul's end was a terrible one. Threatened from all sides and feeling himself abandoned by God, he seemed to have become completely mad. Samuel was dead, so Saul could no longer go to him for advice and felt himself completely alone. One day while he was traveling through the countryside, Saul was told of a woman who could, it was said, cause the dead to appear. The practice of witchcraft had been absolutely forbidden by God and Saul knew this well, but all the same he went to consult the witch without telling her who he was. She, however, knew him at once and foretold terrible happenings. A ghostly shape appeared in the old woman's cave. Was it perhaps only an image created by the madness of the unhappy Saul? The terrified king cried out, "It is

Samuel!" He heard a voice speaking to him. It told the king that tomorrow he and his sons would be with the old Judge in the grave; the Philistines would attack and would be victorious.

The following day everything happened as had been foretold. The Philistines fell on the Israelite army in the hills and completely destroyed it. Both of Saul's sons were killed and he himself was wounded and taken prisoner; he killed himself by falling on his sword.

From now on, David was the sole king of Israel which he was to rule for thirty-seven years, from 1012 B.C. to 975 B.C. His reign was destined to found the power of Israel, to see the destruction of the enemy in all Palestine, and the first organization of the whole country. David was just thirty years old when Saul's death gave him the throne; he was a man of great goodness and wisdom, as brave as he was prudent.

Having command of the twelve tribes, he now gathered a powerful army for a decisive campaign. His columns attacked the enemy from one end of Chanaan to the other. One after the other the Philistine towns were taken by surprise and fell into his hands. He finally established his rule right to the Mediterranean coastline, and, for their part, the marauders of the desert were also subdued.

Surrounded by the warriors of his personal bodyguard, David was always to be found in the hottest part of the battle and seemed to be invincible. He was visibly under the special protection of the Lord.

Now that he had established order throughout all Palestine, David decided that he must have a capital city, as had the Pharaos and the kings of Babylon. He was particularly attracted by one town, Jebus, which was situated in the heart of the country where several trade routes met. The trouble was that it was held by a Chanaanite tribe and was strongly fortified. David attacked it. The siege was long, and he promised a great reward to whoever would be the first to pierce the defenses of the fortress. A young officer named Joab discovered the underground channel which supplied water to the citadel. Creeping through this with a patrol, he took the defenders by surprise and captured the town.

This was how Jebus came to be the capital of Israel. It was destined to remain the capital for all time, in good days and in evil. It was to be not merely the political capital of the kingdom but the Holy City, the center above all others of the religion of the True God. David bestowed a splendid name on his capital: he called it Jerusalem, which means "the abode of peace." In order to dedicate it to God, he caused the Ark of the Covenant to be brought there. It was a wonderful occasion when the Ark was formally installed in Jerusalem. There was an immense procession of all the twelve tribes of Israel, led by the Levites carrying the Ark. In front of them went David, dancing in honor of God, and singing psalms of praise to him.

"O Lord, our Lord, how glorious is Your Name over all the earth! You have raised Your Majesty above the heavens. Out of the mouths of little children You have fashioned praise. May Your foes be vanquished by Your power, destroyed and trodden under foot!"

In spite of all this, in spite of his shining virtues, David was only a man, capable of sin. And sin he did, in a very terrible way. Having seen a young and very beautiful woman, he wanted to marry her, although she was already married to one of his army officers. What made matters worse, was that he, as was the custom of the time, already had several wives, whereas his officer had only one. Still worse, in order to get rid of the husband and to marry Bethsabee, David gave orders that the officer be placed in the most dangerous position in battle so that he might be killed. He was, and David then married Bethsabee.

The Lord now ordered a prophet, one of those inspired people who spoke in God's name, to seek out the king and to charge him with his crime.

Nathan forthwith went to the palace and told the king, "There lived in the city two men; one was very rich and owned immense herds, and the other was very poor and owned just one ewe lamb. In order to make a feast, the rich man stole the poor man's only lamb. What should be done to him?"

The king bounded out of his seat with indignation. "Such a man deserves a terrible punishment. Tell me his name?"

"It is you, King David," replied the prophet. The king understood, and, bowing down humbly before God, he confessed his sin and prayed for forgiveness.

The king, however, had to atone for his sin and to suffer punishment. One of his sons, who was called Absalom, had raised a revolt against him and had enticed away so many of his subjects that David was forced to lead a military expedition gainst his own son. After hard fighting, Absalom was defeated and took refuge in flight, hotly pursued by the king's soldiers. David had ordered his troops to capture his rebel son but, during the pursuit, Absalom's mule bolted under an overhanging tree, and the prince's long hair, flying in the wind, became entangled in the branches. Absalom was thus held hanging by his hair and was killed by one of the king's generals who hated him. David was heartbroken. He had suffered a severe but a just punishment for a grievous sin.

He was seventy years old when he died. Up to the very last moment he had continued to compose Psalms in honor of the Most High, Psalms which were filled with the noblest poetry ever written by man. His people buried him on Mount Sion, in the heart of Jerusalem, the city which he had given to Israel and made holy for all time.

XII

The Splendor and Wisdom of Solomon the Great

"WHAT THEN is this that comes toward us, rising out of the desert like a column of smoke, surrounded by the odor of frankincense and myrrh and of all the spices brought by the caravans from the East?"

It was the litter of Solomon the king, surrounded by sixty of his guards—sixty of the warriors of Israel, skilled in the use of weapons and well trained for battle.

"The King's litter is made of cedar of Libanus; its columns are of silver and its frame of gold. Its seat is of purple velvet embroidered by the loving hands of the maidens of Jerusalem.

"Go forth, O daughters of Sion, to see King Solomon crowned as on his wedding day, and in the day of his joy of heart."

So we have a picture of Solomon, the great king, as he returned to his capital city after a tour of his territories. This splendid procession must have been a magnificent sight, and it is no wonder that the people of Israel said to each other, "Can there be on earth a king so powerful, so rich, so wise as ours? Glory to the son of David!"

For the first time in its history, the small nation which had grown from the twelve tribes found itself governed by a king who in majesty and wealth equaled the Pharaos and the kings of Babylon. And how proud they were of him! Their golden age was to last for barely forty years—from 975 to 935 B.C.—the extent of Solomon's reign, and we can understand how in later years the people cherished the memory of their great king.

When, on his father's death, Solomon knew that he was to be

the ruler of Israel, he had prayed long and earnestly to God. One night the Lord appeared to him and said to him, "Ask what you will of Me."

"Lord," replied the young prince, "give to Your servant an understanding heart, to judge Your people wisely, and to always know good from evil."

God was well pleased with this request and replied, "Because you have asked this thing, I will grant it to you. I will fill your heart with goodness and wisdom so that you shall have no equal on earth. And further, I shall grant you what you have not asked: riches and glory."

As God had promised, so it happened. Everyone was amazed by the goodness and wisdom of the king. People said of him that he knew everything; the name of every plant and animal on earth as well as the answer to every doubt and puzzle that troubled the mind of man. He was also so upright and just that as a judge no one could equal him, and he appeared to have the gift of reading the truth even in the most difficult cases.

For example, one day two women appeared before him with a very difficult problem for him to solve. Both women lived in the same house and both had had a baby at the same time. Accidentally in her sleep one of them had smothered her baby, and, on discovering this, had stolen her neighbor's child, leaving the dead body of her own in its place. Now both women claimed the surviving child and Solomon had to decide which of them was the real mother.

Calling one of his guards he said to him, "Cut the living baby in two, and give half to each woman."

When she heard this order, the real mother was shaken with horror. "No, Sire," she cried, "give the child to the other woman, but do not have it killed!"

So, in his wisdom did Solomon discover the truth and, needless to say, he restored the baby to the woman who by her speech had revealed that she was the real mother.

The Arabs, who greatly admired Solomon, tell another story about him. One day three brothers came to the king and said to him, "When our father lay dying he told us that only one of us was his real son, and so we want you to decide which of us is to inherit his property." The king ordered that the dead body of the father be brought to him and bound upright to a pillar. "Now," he said to the young men, "each of you will shoot an arrow at the dead man's heart, and he who shoots best will be his inheritor." When the turn of one of the young men came he threw away his bow, crying out, "I will not shoot at my father's body."

"All his property is yours," cried the king. "The blood within you has spoken and you have shown yourself a true son."

We see then how well God kept his word to endow Solomon with the gift of wisdom. Nor was He slow to fulfill the second part of His promise. Solomon indeed became powerful and rich, and we should admit that he made full use of his own natural ability to secure this position.

Thanks to his father, who had completed the conquest of Chanaan, Solomon had no enemies to fight. His reign was a peaceful one and all dealings with his neighbors were settled by peaceful methods. He was on such good terms with the Pharao of Egypt that he married one of the King's daughters. He even managed to get on well with the ever restless desert tribes. He also had many great friends among an interesting small nation called the Phenicians, whose country was not far from Palestine.

These Phenicians were a branch of the Semite race, and they had settled along the coast of what we now call Syria, about the year 2800 B.C. The Syrian coastline, being deeply indented, provided good harbors, while the nearby uplands of Libanus grew magnificent forests of cedar which were unequaled for shipbuilding.

So the Phenicians took to the sea, and what magnificent sailors they were! They undertook tremendous voyages in their little blunt-bowed ships, driven by oars or square sails rigged to a single mast, and steered only by two long oars astern. Knowing nothing of compass or sextant, they had navigated not merely the entire Mediterranean Sea, but had voyaged as far north as England and the Baltic Sea, and south to the Gulf of Guinea in Africa. Their seaports of Byblos, Tyre, and Sidon were the greatest trade centers of the period, trading in copper from Cyprus, tin from Cornwall, furs from Russia, textiles from Asia Minor; timber, perfumes, spices—all were there. And it was these same

Phenicians who, for convenience in their trading affairs, had simplified the complicated writing systems of Egypt and Mesopotamia, and had developed the twenty-six signs for vowels and consonants that is the alphabet we use today.

These people were Solomon's greatest friends, in particular, Hiram, king of Tyre. From Hiram, Solomon bought all sorts of goods, selling him in exchange corn, fruit, and oil. From him also he borrowed architects to plan his buildings, and craftsmen to build ships. Solomon had his own fleet which sailed to far-off countries in search of gold, rare perfumes, precious woods, and costly materials. His people established a seaport of their own on the Red Sea. At the same time the king organized a system of caravans which crossed the desert to Mesopotamia and even to India in search of rare merchandise. The people of Jerusalem were astonished to find for the first time in their shops and markets all sorts of new things: trinkets of gold and ivory, boxes of sweet-scented sandalwood from India, even monkeys, parrots, and peacocks.

Solomon devoted a great part of the riches which he acquired by his skill in commerce to a holy and glorious purpose: the building of a Temple to the Lord God. Up till now the people of Israel had no place of worship comparable to the pagan temples on the Nile or Euphrates. The simple Ark of the Covenant, the sacred chest that contained the Tablets of the Law, was the tabernacle of their Invisible God. And for the gatherings of the worshippers, had they not the hills and the plains and all the beauties of nature that came from God Himself? Now, however, that Israel was a prosperous kingdom, it was fitting that it should build a monument to God that would be worthy of its faith and of its riches.

Therefore, as a site for the Temple, Solomon chose a rocky eminence in Jerusalem facing the citadel of Sion and called Mount Moria. It was already holy ground for it was here (do you not remember?) that Abraham had brought his son Isaac for sacrifice at the command of God. By dint of immense labor the hill was shaped, and the surface leveled. With the help of a supporting wall, the workers constructed at the summit a splendid platform, 1500 feet long by over 800 feet in width, from which there now began to rise the walls of the Temple.

Rare stones and marbles, precious woods and metals, nothing was spared in this great enterprise. The plans for the Temple were drawn up by the Tyrian architects lent by King Hiram. A hundred and fifty thousand men labored for seven years at the building. When it was completed, the Temple was truly worthy of the Lord and Master of heaven and earth. It was approached by a ramp leading to the first courtyard, open to the faithful at all times. A second inner wall marked the enclosure of the priests. Finally, enclosed by a third wall, was the Temple itself, the sanctuary. It was not very large—thirty-six feet by one hundred and thirty—but it was unbelievably magnificent.

In truth, the Temple was a masterpiece of beauty! The air was laden with the sweet fragrance of the cedar, sandalwood, and cypress with which the walls were paneled. How the gold on the sacred ornaments glittered, and how the light winked and flashed on the ten great hanging lamps! The great veil of the Temple, made of pure linen embroidered in purple and gold, fell in a noble sweep across the entrance to the "Holy of Holies" where rested the Ark of the Covenant. Most impressive of all were the angels, the two cherubim in gilded wood; in the incense-scented interior they seemed to keep an eternal vigil of prayer to the Most High.

There were, of course, no statues in the Temple. The Lord Himself had forbidden Moses to allow any image to be made lest people should associate such an image with the idols of Egypt and Chaldea. The True God is not visible. Statues were not needed in order to adore Him; for He is present in the innermost heart of those who pray to Him. And so, in the very heart of Solomon's sanctuary there were only the two Tablets of the Law, the Decalogue given by God to Moses on Mount Sinai as the expression of His Will.[1]

The Temple was not the only great building erected by Solomon. He also built a vast palace, containing great pillared halls, a fortress, storehouses, water cisterns, and innumerable other things. It would be impossible to list all the great buildings that Solomon caused to spring up. The only comparison that we can find in the modern world is the vast palace of Versailles, near Paris, erected by the great King Louis XIV as a monument to the glory of his reign. So did Solomon's buildings celebrate for all time the glory of the great Israelite king.

One day an especially splendid caravan approached Jerusalem. A long file of camels carried personages whose costume and complexion revealed that they had come from a far-distant land. In their baggage were great quantities of gold, precious stones, and costly spices. Even down to the trappings and harness of their mounts, everything was magnificent. It was the Queen of Saba who had come with her retinue from her little-known kingdom in the depths of Arabia to see Solomon for herself, so much had she heard about him. The two monarchs exchanged presents, and discussed many things with great wisdom. Then the visiting queen took her departure, singing the praises of Solomon's wisdom and glory. Israel was overcome with astonishment at the splendors displayed during her visit.

Earthly glory, alas, does not last for long, and all too often great states collapse at the moment of their greatest glory. Great wealth has many dangers, and the greatest of them all is sinful pride. It is

[1] With the coming of Christianity, this fear of idol worship was gradually to disappear. Symbols and paintings were used by the earliest Christians for the instruction and edification of the faithful. The Council of Trent makes clear the Church's teaching regarding the use of statues and pictures of Christ, the Virgin Mary, the saints and other sacred subjects: they are to be given due honor and veneration "not because it is believed that any divinity or virtue is in them, or that anything may be asked from them or that any confidence can be placed in the images themselves as was done of old by the Gentiles . . . but because the honor shown to them is directed to those whom they represent."

true that up to his dying day Solomon never swerved from his faith in the True God or ceased to pray to Him; but he did perhaps take too much pleasure in his glory and power. Did he forget that everything he had came from the hands of God? Further, his gigantic building plans cost a very great deal. To pay for them he had to levy heavy taxes on his people, and to demand forced labor from them. The Israelites grew discontented to the point of open rebellion. Here again we can compare Solomon to Louis XIV of France. Both monarchs grew overproud and ruined themselves with their grandiose building plans, so that the end of their reigns were clouded by gloom. . . .

Solomon, moreover, committed an even more grievous sin. He had numerous wives, and among them were many foreigners who had brought with them their own false gods. So it was that in Jerusalem itself, the Holy City of the Lord, the king's Egyptian wife worshipped the cow-headed divinity of Egypt, his Phenician wife worshipped Baal, and his other pagan wives each worshipped her own false god. Such an insult to the One True God could but be deserving of punishment.

But God, Who knows the hearts of men, permitted these things to happen. The collapse of his kingdom was to follow quickly on Solomon's death, but even this collapse was to have its purpose: to hasten the fulfillment of the mission which, since the days of Abraham, had been the destiny of the people of Israel.

XIII
The Prophets of Israel

The Bible tells us that, "Pride goes before a fall, and vanity leads to disaster." This proverb applies as much to nations as it does to individuals. Solomon was hardly in his grave when his proud little kingdom was split in two. His son Roboam had, by bad statesmenship, brought about a rebellion among the ten tribes who occupied northern Palestine, and he could not subdue them. These ten tribes declared that henceforth they would form an independent kingdom, and would no longer obey the king of Jerusalem, so that the latter now governed only the two tribes that occupied Judea in the south (see map on front endpaper) of the country.

To understand the situation, it was as though all except the New England States seceded from the Union, or all England except the Home countries refused allegiance to the Crown and showed itself more or less hostile to it. In the case of Israel it was even worse, for Palestine was such a small country that the separate kingdoms were mere statelets, quite unable to defend themselves against their enemies. This was no time for weakness, since a terrible threat had appeared from the East. The whole of Mesopotamia was falling into the hands of the Assyrians. No doubt you have read in your school books of these fierce people. They were Semites, and therefore of the same race as the Chaldeans and the Hebrews, but they were mountaineers from the Upper Euphrates and knew only one trade—war. In this they were remarkably successful. Their army was the finest in the world, consisting of heavily-armored infantry, light infantry, and engineers expert in siege operations. They lacked nothing in the way of equipment and their war chariots, with scythe blades attached to their wheels, were formidable weapons in attack. Even rivers could not halt them, for each soldier carried a leather float that could be blown up and on which he could paddle to the other side.

This powerful army had a well-deserved reputation for barbarity. Wherever the Assyrians went they left nothing but ruins and dead bodies behind them. They inflicted all sorts of horrible tortures on their prisoners, impaling them on stakes, gouging out their eyes, tearing out their tongues and nails, and, worst horror of all, burning them alive. On a monument which he erected, one of their kings inscribed the boast that he had built a pyramid of ten thousand human heads.

At the very moment when Israel split into two fragments, the Assyrians, having completed the conquest of Mesopotamia, were beginning to look toward the Mediterranean, saying to themselves that it would be a good idea to seize the small countries that lay along the coast. And, as if this was not enough for Israel, Egypt had now settled down from its internal struggles and planned again to occupy Palestine, which meant that fierce battles would take place between Egyptian and Assyrian forces on Chanaanite soil. In the face of this terrible danger, the chosen people were thinking only of their own disputes.

So it was that the three centuries following Solomon's death were disastrous ones for Israel. Time after time there was savage war between the two kingdoms, wars between brothers who had become enemies. They only fought off attacks by Egypt or the desert Bedouins in order to fight more fiercely against each other. The northern tribes wished to establish their capital at Samaria (see map on front endpaper), which was a slight against Jerusalem. In both kingdoms crisis followed crisis, and there were a succession of rebellions and revolutions. For example, Samaria had eight different royal dynasties in two hundred years.

Even this was not the worst. There was something far more grave. The descendants of Abraham and of Moses became false to the religion of the True God. As they mixed more and more with the local people, they began little by little to accept their idols. The kings of Samaria and Jerusalem continued, like Solomon, to marry foreigners, and these stranger queens brought their own forms of idolatry with them.

Before long there were many altars to the Phenician God Baal throughout the Promised Land. Also there were statues of the Golden Calf of Egypt. It was not a pretty sight, particularly as the ceremonies that went along with this idol worship were revolting and horrible. The followers of Baal, also known as Moloch, made human sacrifice to him, and even burned young children alive before his image.

The chosen people had indeed fallen low! And, as you can well imagine, the consequences of their wrongdoing were disastrous. Those who remained faithful to the Lord would have nothing to do with these abominable pagan rites, and this was yet another cause of strife. Here, for example, are the stories of two pagan queens, both of whose lives ended in tragedy.

The first was called Jezabel, and she was the wife of Achab, king of Samaria. Born a Phenician princess, Jezabel had not only established the worship of the Baal of Tyre in the Land of Chanaan, but she even persecuted the priests of the true religion. Apart from this, both she and her husband were cruel and oppressive rulers. One day, for instance, they wanted to enlarge their personal domains by adding to it the vineyard of a very upright and honest man, so they caused him to be accused and put to death on false evidence.

Her crimes called down a terrible punishment on Jezabel. Inspired by God, one of the generals of her army, a believer in the True God, rebelled against her rule. Descending upon the capital, he captured it. From the balcony of the palace, the queen watched the entry of the rebel.

"Murderer!" she cried.

"Throw her over the balcony," ordered the victorious general, and so it was done. The bleeding body of Jezabel fell on the flag stones where it was mangled by stray dogs.

Jezabel's daughter, Athalia, fared no better. She was married to a king of Jerusalem, and had great influence over this weak man. After his death she was afraid of being dethroned by one of her grandchildren, and so she had the entire royal family put to death. She too, of course, was a pagan and had brought her false gods into the Holy City itself. But the priests of the Lord were watching. They had succeeded in saving from the massacre the little Prince Joas, last survivor of the royal line. The people rose against Athalia. She tried to seek refuge in the Temple, but the soldiers found her and she perished under their swords.

What a scene of blood and horror was offered by Israel at this time! Had God forsaken His people, allowing them to sink deeper and deeper into sin and to bring about their destruction by their own hands? As you know, God has created man an absolutely free being. He has given them laws and explained the difference between right and wrong. If, after all this, men fall into sin, they bring their punishment on their own heads. But often, in His mercy, God forgives them and spares them if only they repent. So it happened with the people of Israel.

Perhaps also there was another motive behind the decrees of Providence. Had the kingdom of Solomon survived, becoming all the time more and more wealthy and powerful, the results might have been remarkably different from the role which God had decided for Israel. The chosen people might have ended by thinking only of money and conquest. This was not the destiny for which God had intended them. Misfortune teaches people to think and to try to become better. When good times return, they think only about amusing themselves.

You have no doubt already noticed how throughout the long history of Israel, there appeared from time to time men gifted with extraordinary powers who seemed to see into the future and to foretell what was going to happen; men who seemed to interpret the Will of God. Moses was one such man, and he had spoken to his people in the name of the Most High. There were many others, and one of the most remarkable features of the remarkable history of Israel is the presence of these great men who were the bearers of God's Word on earth and who did so much to develop the true religion among the chosen people.

In the grave period in which Israel now found itself, such figures appeared particularly often. They were called "Prophets," which means, "those who speak in the name of God." We do not know just how many there were of these men. There were certainly sixteen, for their teachings are recorded in the Bible, but there is no doubt that there were many more. They were drawn from all classes of society. One was a simple herdsman and another a wealthy nobleman; others came from the priesthood and even from the royal family. The Spirit of God breathes where It wills and inspires whom It wills.

Try to make a picture for yourself of these men as they went about their mission. Some dressed in strange clothing, covering themselves with coarse goatskins or the skin of other animals, using a rough cord as belt, and going barefooted. Others dressed in more ordinary fashion. But they all had one thing in common —unbelievable courage and daring. They spoke in the Name of God, and so they feared no one, neither the popular mob nor persons in high places; not even the kings themselves, to whom they never hesitated to tell the truth they were charged to tell. (You will remember how the prophet Nathan rebuked David for his sin.) Threats, blows, even death—and there were some of them who died under torture—meant nothing to them. God had commanded them to speak, and so they spoke.

What had they to say? At first they all repeated the great truth that Israel was the nation of God, the Lord's witness upon earth; that the ancient Covenant still held and that the chosen people had a great destiny before it. We see, however, how in the course of the four centuries when the Prophets were most numerous the burden of their message changed.

At first, their message was always one of warning of terrible dangers to come. They chided the rich for their pride and selfishness, the poor for their lack of faith, and the entire people for their disobedience to the commandments of God. They foretold dire disasters which would come upon the people as just punishment for their sins.

"You are murderers, unruly and untruthful, always forgetful of My commandments. You even worship false gods. But beware! My day will come, the day of wrath, when I shall unloose upon you a horde of enemies and in your cities they will not leave a stone upon a stone."

Later on, when their prophecy had been fulfilled and God's anger had abated, the Prophets' mission was to explain to the people the reason for the disasters that had overtaken them. Their misfortunes were a punishment, a terrible but fully deserved punishment, for what they had done. What they had to do now was to repent of their sins, and ask God's pardon so that He should show them mercy.

Later still, as we shall see, when Israel had reached the very depth of her misery, there were Prophets who spoke words of consolation to the people: "Take courage, you chosen people! He who has chastised you will not let you perish and He has taken pity on your sufferings. He will make a new Covenant with you and, once you have realized your wrongdoings, your repentance will bring its own reward."

You will see from this the importance of the part played by the Prophets. It was thanks to them that the religion of Israel developed in such a manner as to become the forerunner of Christianity. One of the Prophets told the people, "You sacrifice animals to God, but are you any the better for it? God prefers good deeds to any sacrifice and the true way of pleasing Him is to live in purity, justice, and charity." Other Prophets declared that the poor, the oppressed, and all who suffered injustice, were the friends of God and one day He would comfort them. The Prophets said many other fine and noble things, all of which we know to have been true.

Let us take a closer look at three of these majestic figures, for they are well worthy of study.

At the time when Achab and Jezabel ruled over Samaria, the prophet Elias appeared before them. He condemned them for their idolatry and foretold their dire punishment. A terrible drought came which lasted for three and a half years so that the entire populace was starving to death. After delivering his message to the rulers of the land, Elias had vanished and, guided by the Lord, had betaken himself to the side of a brook where ravens appeared morning and evening, bringing him food. Achab made fruitless efforts to

find Elias, and at length the prophet himself decided to appear again before him. Achab bitterly reproached him as the cause of the misfortunes of the country.

"Now," mocked Elias, "is the time to call on your false gods to help you. Have two altars made ready and let the priests of Baal make their sacrifice on one while I make mine on the other. We shall then both ask God to show His power by lighting the sacrificial fire beneath one of them."

So it was done, and the priests of Baal prayed to their idol, dancing, chanting and imploring his aid; but all in vain, for nothing happened. Scarcely, however, had Elias commenced his prayer to the Lord God than there was a great peal of thunder, and a flash of lightning set woodpile and victims in flames. That same evening, a rain cloud appeared in the sky. . . .

It was again Elias who, when he heard of the vineyard that had been stolen by the king and queen, upbraided them for their action and foretold the punishment that was about to fall on them. The Bible tells us that God had such love for this faithful and gallant servant that He even exempted him from the law that decrees that all men must die. One day, when Elias was walking in the country accompanied by his disciple Eliseus, they suddenly saw approaching them a fiery chariot drawn by fiery horses. Elias mounted the chariot and was carried up to heaven in a whirlwind.

Later on, another great prophet came on the scene, this time in Jerusalem. A man named Isaias was engaged in meditation in the Temple, when he went into a state of ecstasy and God appeared to him. The air was filled with six-winged angels who sang a song (which we hear to this day): "Holy, Holy, Holy, is the Lord God of hosts. All the earth is full of Thy glory."

Isaias was overcome by his vision and asked himself, "What is going to become of me? I am a sinner, a poor sinner whose lips are unclean from his sins?"

But even as he said this, one of the angels flew to him and taking a burning coal from the brazier on the altar, he touched his mouth with it saying, "Your sins are forgiven. Now go and speak to the people in the Name of the Lord."

So Isaias went forth to the market squares, to the villages and to the towns. His eloquence was wonderful and huge crowds used to gather to hear him. The power of God seemed even more terrible when he spoke of it, and he foretold the future with incredible accuracy. He foresaw the invasion of Chanaan by the Assyrian armies, the destruction of Samaria, and the scattering of its people —all Israel was going to suffer for its sins.

"The ox knows his owner, and the ass his master's crib: but Israel does not know Me, and does not want to know me. O, sinful nation, what will be your end if you continue to revolt?" These words fell like a whiplash on Isaias' hearers. Some of them listened, repented their sins, and changed their way of life. Many others, however, just shrugged their shoulders and said, "He is mad!" or even threatened the prophet with violence.

Finally, just as the catastrophe was about to take place, still another great voice rang through Israel, that of the prophet Jeremias. He appeared in mourning garb, his garments torn and his head covered with ashes, uttering most terrible words as though he saw before his very eyes the tragedy that was about to commence. "I tremble with fear and can no longer keep silence. What is this terrible trumpet call? Destruction upon destruction; our country is laid waste. Tents, houses—all are destroyed."

So we see that just at the moment when Israel was about to be overwhelmed by misfortune, the Prophets reminded her people of two things: that their misery would be the bitter fruit of their sins, but that if they repented they could win back the mercy of God.

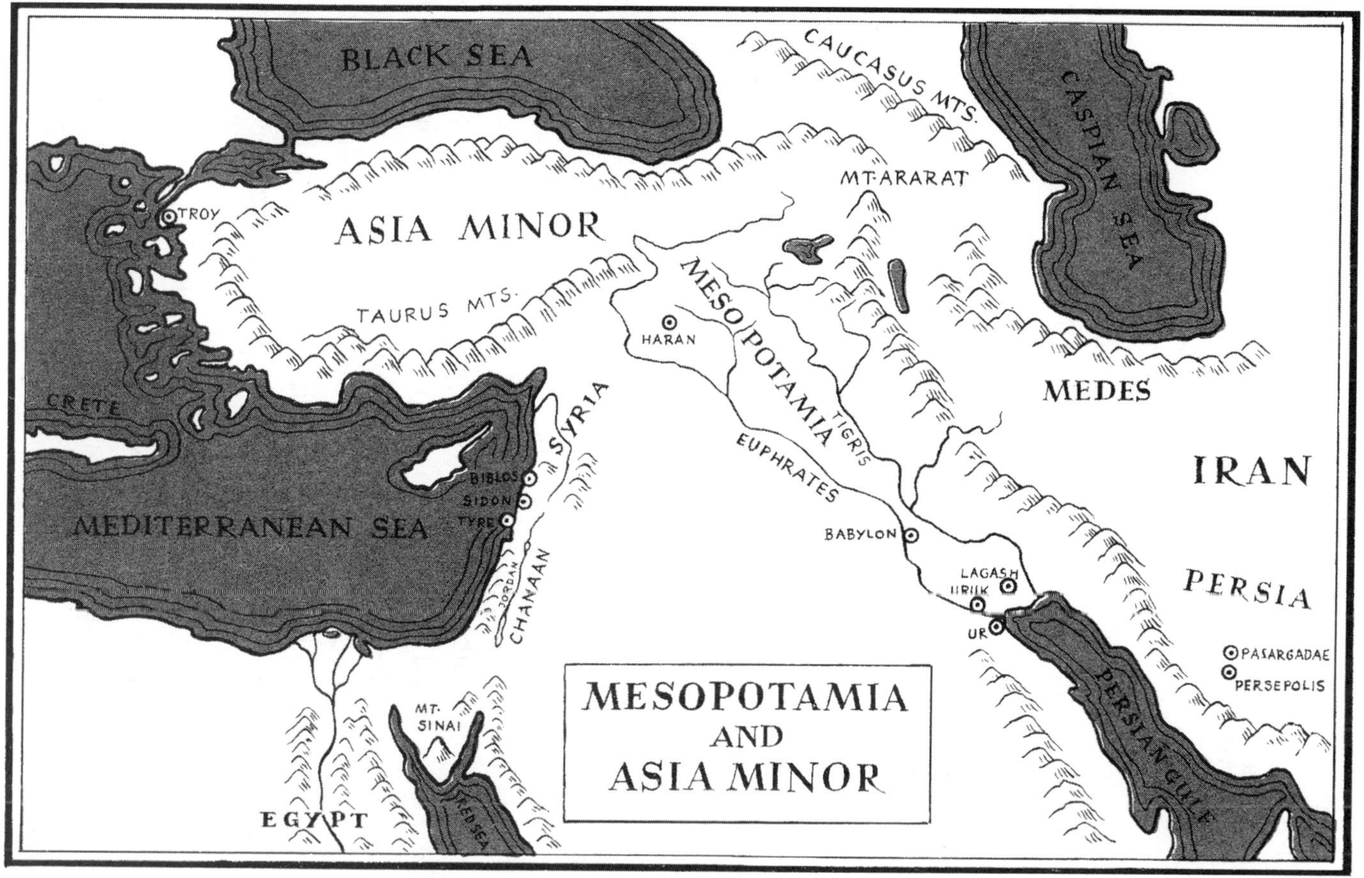
MESOPOTAMIA
AND
ASIA MINOR
BLACK SEA
CASPIAN SEA
CAUCASUS MTS.
MT. ARARAT
ASIA MINOR
TROY
TAURUS MTS.
MESOPOTAMIA
HARAN
TIGRIS
EUPHRATES
MEDES
IRAN
PERSIA
PASARGADAE
PERSEPOLIS
BABYLON
LAGASH
URUK
UR
PERSIAN GULF
CRETE
MEDITERRANEAN SEA
SYRIA
BIBLOS
SIDON
TYRE
JORDAN
CHANAAN
MT. SINAI
RED SEA
EGYPT

XIV

Dark Days for Israel: Exile in Babylon

It was in the year 745 (B.C. of course; see note at the end of this book) that the fierce Assyrian warriors made their first appearance on the hills and plains of Palestine. On every road their helmets and breastplates glittered in the sun and everywhere their path was marked by the usual atrocities. What had happened? This terrible misfortune was due to the fact that once again war had broken out between the two Hebrew kingdoms that had become such deadly enemies of one another. Samaria had attempted to subdue Judea, and the latter country had committed the unpardonable crime of appealing for help to Assyria. It was as though in some dispute in a Western nation one of the parties had sought the support of the Russians.

Sargon, the greatest of the Assyrian military leaders, blockaded Samaria and captured it after a savage siege. Then, as he himself boasted, he deported 27,290 people to his own country as slaves, replacing them by more or less idolatrous pagans drawn from all parts, and demolishing the walls of the city. As for the kingdom of Judea, it gained little profit from its evil deed for it not only had to pay tribute to the conqueror but lived in constant fear of the Assyrian soldiery, now stationed only a few miles from its borders. By the year 722 B.C., the kingdom of Samaria had completely disappeared, while the kingdom of Jerusalem was to survive it for a century and a half, until 586 B.C.

In spite of all this, God did not abandon His people. It is proved by the fact that it was at this very time that Isaias, perhaps the greatest and most admirable of all the Hebrew Prophets, lived and taught. When we read his prophecies we are struck by the beauty of his words and the splendor of his style, for he was not only a prophet inspired by God but a magnificent poet. His message to the people was, above all, that God is All Powerful and that we are all in His hands. Playing at politics and making of alliances meant nothing: all that mattered was to believe in God and to obey Him. "If you do not believe, you cannot live. Our only strength lies in our belief in God."

In addition to this message, cries of grief came from the lips of Isaias, for he knew the faults of his fellow countrymen only too well. "I have cherished my children and they have rebelled against me." Isaias foretold terrible punishment that would fall on Israel if his people did not mend their ways. "Cease to do evil," he said. "Seek justice and your sins will be pardoned; even if they be scarlet, God will make you white as snow." But Israel refused to listen or to understand, and not even the clearest signs of God's goodwill could restrain his people from falling back into sin.

In the year 701, a new Assyrian king found an excuse to pick a quarrel with the little kingdom of Judea and sent his armies against Jerusalem. The outlook seemed hopeless for the defenders, for the besiegers were terribly strong in numbers. But suddenly the Assyrians broke off the siege and vanished toward the south to meet the threat of a hostile army from Egypt. Nothing more was heard of them until one day messengers came crying out, "Rejoice, O people of Jerusalem, the Assyrians are all dead, a hundred and forty thousand of them! The plague struck their camp and not one of them has escaped."

By this means God had given His people cause for fear, to show them that their fate lay in His hands. The prophecy of Isaias was fulfilled, but he did not rejoice for he doubted if the people would learn from experience. Would they have the wisdom to understand the lesson that had been taught them and to reform their ways? They did in fact reform, but their good behavior did not last for long. The good king Josias restored the worship of the Lord in its former purity. Happily, just at this moment, a chance discovery in the Temple revealed a scroll containing the greater portion of the law of Moses, which the people studied with great care. At about this time also the Assyrian Empire fell into a state of great disorder, for, like all peoples who rule others by force, the Assyrians were hated by everyone. A great alliance was formed against them: Ninive, their capital city, was captured. Exactly as Isaias had foretold, the cruel tyranny collapsed, and the people of Jerusalem thought that they were safe again.

They were, alas, completely wrong. Mesopotamia fell under the rule of the Babylonians, led by their great king, Nabuchodonosor. The Babylonians were just as unpleasant to deal with as the Assyrians. They too had their terrible armies; they too wanted to establish themselves on the Mediterranean coast. The threat to Jerusalem was as grave as ever.

All this time the people of Jerusalem could find nothing better to do than to argue and bicker among themselves. Josias' successor was a man of little ability, and it was suggested that Judea should form an alliance with Egypt against Babylon, which would have been like a dog and a mouse combining to fight a tiger. To make matters worse, the people fell into their old sinful ways, were unfaithful to God, and disobeyed His commandments.

Again, however, there appeared on the scene a man who had a wonderful understanding of all these tragic happenings: the great prophet Jeremias. One can but be moved at the thought of this witness who spoke in the Name of the Most High, who missed nothing of the tragedy that was about to overwhelm his country, whose warnings, protests, and appeals were all in vain and who had to stand by and watch the evil deeds of his people draw down the anger of heaven upon themselves. In the face of their squabbles and political intrigues, he could not restrain himself from telling them, "All this counts for nothing! You are about to be vanquished and your towns destroyed. All you who adore false gods, who care for nothing but worldly wealth, whose hearts are filled with evil, your punishment is at hand." Nevertheless,

Jeremias did not despair of Israel. On the contrary, he foretold in the Name of God that Babylon in its turn would be destroyed, and that once again God would have mercy on His chosen people when they had returned to their faith in Him.

The prophecies of Jeremias were soon fulfilled exactly. For the first time Nabuchodonosor besieged the Holy City in 591 B.C., captured it and sent the king, the royal family, and many other Israelites into exile. Later on, learning that the people were still plotting against him, he returned, determined this time to teach them a terrible lesson.

And a truly terrible lesson it was. Attacked by a ferocious enemy, the people of Jerusalem shut themselves in behind their walls and defended the city for eighteen months. Food supplies ran out, and it is said that some of the starving defenders were driven to the point

of eating dead human bodies. Then the plague broke out in the Holy City and wrought terrible havoc.

In the end Jerusalem was forced to surrender. The infuriated Babylonians broke in, pillaging, burning, and killing at random. The Temple, the wonderful Temple of Solomon, went up in flames and the Ark of the Covenant was destroyed. Half of the city was razed to the ground. With his own hands Nabuchodonosor put out the eyes of the last king of Israel. Then he gave orders that all the rich and well-educated people and the Levites were to be brought as hostages back to the Euphrates country.

This terrible disaster took place in 586 B.C., three and a half centuries after the death of Solomon. Now, before we follow our poor Israelites in their exile, let us pause for a moment to consider what was happening in the rest of the world while these events were taking place in Palestine, in the small province of Judea. It would be wrong to think that history can be divided into compartments or that one can learn the history of one people without considering that of others. You have, no doubt, been told in school about the founding of Rome by Romulus, and you remember how Romulus and Remus were nursed by a she-wolf. Well, this foundation of Rome probably took place in 753 B.C., that is, about the same time as the destruction of Samaria. You have also, of course, heard of the great Greek poet, Homer, the author of the *Iliad,* the epic of the siege of Troy, and of the *Odyssey,* the story of the adventures of Ulysses. Homer lived in Asia Minor at the same time as the prophet Isaias lived in Palestine.

Now let us follow these unhappy Israelites as they wind their way into exile along the desert trails. Truly, their fate has been tragic. They have seen the death of thousands of their people, and have watched their houses and their property go up in flames. All they have been able to save are such a few poor odds and ends as they have been able to load on their pack animals. Now they stagger along under the burning Syrian sun. If they falter, Nabuchodonosor's soldiers lash them with whips as if they are dogs, and if anyone falls sick he is killed without mercy. The leaders of the people are treated even more cruelly: a ring, through which passes a rope, is fixed in their lips, and thus in groups of four or five they are tethered like pigs to the saddle of a Babylonian horseman.

At last, in the depth of their great misery, the chosen people turned back to God. Now they know how right were their Prophets in their ceaseless warnings of punishment to come. They have sinned; now they were being chastised and all that is left for them to do is to pray God to forgive them. And, however grave their sins, it must be put to the credit of the people of Israel that they could always find sublime words in which to express their repentance. So it is that to this very day we sing the magnificent hymn of grief and hope which expresses the agony of Israel on her way to exile. It is known in Latin as the *De Profundis:*

> Out of the depths I have cried to thee,
> O Lord: Lord, hear my voice.
>
> Let thy ears be attentive to the voice
> of my supplication.
> If thou, O Lord, wilt mark iniquities:
> Lord, who shall stand it.
> For with thee there is merciful for-
> giveness: and by reason of thy law, I
> have waited for thee, O Lord.
>
> My soul hath relied on his word: my
> soul hath hoped in the Lord.
> From the morning watch even until
> night, let Israel hope in the Lord.
> Because with the Lord there is mercy:
> and with him plentiful redemption.
> And he shall redeem Israel from all
> his iniquities.

Babylon was reached at last. With tear-drenched eyes the exiles gazed at this powerful city which they could not have failed to admire had their fate been less unhappy. They marveled at the colossal ramparts, so vast that it took a fifteen hours march to encircle them, at the great five-arched bridge, at the lofty many-storied temples, at the royal palace with its hundreds of apartments, and, above all, at the famous "Hanging Gardens of Babylon." These were made up of terrace above terrace of trees and rare plants, with waterfalls and fountains. It was all very beautiful, but the poor prisoners got no benefit from this display of luxury.

At first the Israelites, like their ancestors of old in Egypt, were set to forced labor, making bricks and building houses, exposed all the time to the sun and to the whips of the overseers. Then, gradually, the iron hand of the Babylonians relaxed. The Israelites were allowed to settle in a district of their own, where they were permitted to build villages and to till the soil. Some of them became traders and bankers and, as the Hebrew people have always been highly intelligent, we soon see them becoming officials of the king of Babylon.

Even so, life was sad and painful for them. The worst part of exile is the separation from one's native land. Where now was the former splendor of Israel, the glory of Solomon? Throughout this sixth century B.C., many other peoples were growing in riches and culture. This was the time when Croesus, whose name remains a symbol of great wealth, ruled as king in Asia Minor: when, in Africa, the Phenicians, who had founded Carthage, were making their city into one of the greatest seaports of the Mediterranean. Its rival was Marseilles in Gaul, founded by the Greeks, and now at the height of its prosperity. While all this development was taking place, the Israelites pined in a strange country, far from the holy land which God had promised them. So, from the very heart of these people, so gifted in poetry, there flowed another glorious psalm of grief and faith in God:

> Upon the rivers of Babylon, there we
> sat and wept: when we remembered
> Sion:

> On the willows in the midst thereof we hung up our instruments. For there they that led us into captivity required of us the words of songs.
>
> And they that carried us away, said: Sing ye to us a hymn of the songs of Sion.
>
> How shall we sing the song of the Lord in a strange land?
>
> If I forget thee, O Jerusalem, let my right hand be forgotten.
>
> Let my tongue cleave to my jaws, if I do not remember thee:
>
> If I make not Jerusalem the beginning of my joy.

But in their sad plight as exiles, God did not forget His people. On the contrary, He sent them Prophets to console them and to make them understand the reason for their sufferings.

Jeremias was dead. At the moment when disaster overtook them, his people hated him for having accused them so openly of their sins and for having so clearly foretold the evils that were about to befall them. In their rage some wicked people had thrown the prophet into an empty water cistern. This time he was delivered from certain death, but after that he was continually persecuted and in the end he was killed.

The Most High, however, sent other Prophets to keep up the courage of His people. The Bible tells us of these Prophets of the captivity. In the second half of the Book of Isaias, we can read the message of forgiveness and hope which assured Israel of the continuing protection of God. Now there came upon the scene another prophet named Ezechiel; he again told the chosen people that if they repented of their sins, God would forgive them, would allow them to return to Palestine, and would restore the former glory of Israel. Hope would come through repentance!

This was the repeated message of the Prophets of the captivity. And we can well understand how, having suffered so sorely under

God's anger, the people listened with obedience to these mighty voices speaking in the Name of the Lord:

"The Lord God is angry because men no longer practice justice and because truth has disappeared. We have lived in discord and rebellion; we have denied our God. Our sins cry out against us, and God has armed Himself for vengeance. Each one of us has been paid according to his merits, and every sin shall have its punishment!

"But God's Covenant with His people still remains: I will forgive whoever repents his sins. Arise, O Jerusalem, and let thy splendor shine anew, for once again thy light shall shine over the nations. Thy children will regain their native land; the Temple of God shall rise again and once again Israel shall be happy and respected by all."

So spoke Isaias and, after him, Ezechiel repeated the same message while telling of the strange vision which came to him. On one occasion, for example, he had seen in a vision an immense plain covered with dry bones. Then God spoke, and lo! these dry skeletons came to life, flesh returned to their bones, skin covered the flesh, and the dead were restored to life.

It is easy to understand the meaning of this vision. The dry bones represented the unhappy Israelites in exile, while those restored to life represented a liberated people happily restored to their Promised Land under the blessing of the Omnipotent God.

XV

Stories of the Babylonian Captivity

WHEN THE FORTUNES of a nation take a bad turn its people turn for comfort to the memories of happier times and like to recall the gallant and noble figures of their past history. In the grim years when most of Europe lay under the heel of Germany, the minds of the French turned to St. Louis, to St. Joan of Arc who freed France from foreign invaders, to Napoleon and to their heroes of the first World War. The Poles thought of Sobieski and Kosciusko, the Dutch of William the Silent and so on.

So it was with the Israelites. As dusk fell on the exiled villages scattered along the banks of the Euphrates, the old stories of the fatherland and of the True God were told and retold and helped to maintain hope in the hearts of the people.

Here, for example, is one of these stories, the adventures of an heroic young woman called Judith.

At the time when Nabuchodonosor was leading his armies across Palestine to attack Jerusalem, one of the Judean cities was besieged by the fierce Babylonians and the situation in the town soon became desperate. Food supplies were running out and even the water supply was about to fail, as the attackers had cut off the supply. It was in vain that the High Priest Eliachim, a man of great piety and energy, tried to whip up the courage of his fellow citizens, telling them unceasingly, "Fast and pray and leave the rest to God." It soon became clear that no assistance could be looked for, and already some people were speaking of surrender.

It was at this moment that a young and very handsome woman, a widow called Judith, who was held up as an example of perfect character and piety, came on the scene and sought out the leaders of the city. She offered to go herself to the camp of the enemy general. When asked what her plans were, she replied that if she were allowed to have her way these would soon be revealed.

Dressed in her best finery, perfumed and bedecked with earrings and necklaces, a fine headdress on her head, Judith made her way to the camp of Holofernes, the enemy general. Barbarian though he was, he wished to be civil to such a beautiful woman, and he invited her to dine with him. This was just what Judith wanted. During the feast, she persuaded Holofernes to drink so much that he did not know what he was doing. At the end of the meal he fell fast asleep. The courageous woman did not hesitate. Seizing his sword which was hanging from a pole of the tent, Judith grasped the drunkard by the hair and cut off his head. She then made her escape under cover of darkness. The following day the defenders displayed Holofernes' head from the walls of the city. The besieging army was terrified at the sight and fled. Judith had saved her city.

Many such stories, all of them teaching us to trust in God above all, are to be found in the Bible. The one that tells of the prophet Jonas is truly remarkable. One day the Voice of the Most High spoke to Jonas, saying, "Arise and go to Ninive and preach to the people, warning them of the punishment that will fall upon them because of their wickedness."

Go to Ninive, the Assyrian capital, and address the people in such terms! One might as well try to teach virtue to a troop of lions or tigers! So thought Jonas, who had no desire to find himself impaled on a stake or to be burned alive. So, instead of setting out for Ninive, he disobeyed God's command and took a ship for Spain.

Now, during the voyage, God sent a terrible storm which threatened to overwhelm the ship. Trembling, Jonas confessed to the crew that it must have been his disobedience that had drawn down God's anger on them. At this the sailors at once seized him and threw him into the sea. Poor Jonas! He had tried to avoid probable death and he now seemed doomed to a certain one.

At the moment, however, when Jonas struck the water, God, who only wished to teach him a severe lesson, sent a gigantic fish, a sort of huge whale, who swallowed the prophet in one gulp. Safe and sound, but very frightened at finding himself in this strange black cavern that was the inside of the whale, Jonas uttered a fervent prayer to God. If his life was spared he would make all haste to carry out the mission imposed on him by the Most High! God then ordered the fish to cast out Jonas; next day the prophet found himself in daylight on a sandy beach on the coast. From there he made haste to teach the law of God in Ninive, just as he had been ordered to do.

Surely the God who had cast Jonas into the abyss and then restored him safely to the light of day, would not do less for His poor people of Israel! They too were in the abyss and waiting to be restored to the light.

This strange story held yet another message for the Jewish people, one that they found very difficult to understand. The message was that the true faith was not intended for the chosen people alone; that it was their duty to teach it to other peoples, to all peoples.

Now here is yet another story, which shows clearly to us the goodness of God to those who love and serve Him faithfully. It is that of Tobias and his journey.

In one of the Israelite village settlements in Mesopotamia there lived a very saintly old man, a devoted servant of the Lord. He was blind, for one day a swallow's droppings had fallen into his eyes. As a result of this accident he was unable to work, and he lived in poverty. His neighbors used to jeer at him, saying, "You prided yourself on being the true servant of God—what do you think of Him now, since He has inflicted such trials on you?" To all these mocking questions the good old man had only one reply: that nothing and nobody could shake his faith in the goodness of God. We shall now see how his confidence was rewarded.

Before he had been overcome by misfortune, the old man had lent a large sum of money to a relative of his who lived far away in the high mountains. Now that he had fallen on evil days this money was sorely needed. He wondered if he should send his son Tobias to collect it. It would mean a long and dangerous journey through country that was filled with outlaws and robbers, and no one was likely to offer to accompany Tobias on such a risky voyage. The young man, however, was eager to make the attempt and finally persuaded his father to allow him to do so.

As Tobias was about to set out, accompanied only by his dog, a good-looking and pleasant-mannered young man came up to him. He said he had learned that both he and Tobias were traveling in the same direction, and suggested that they join forces for the journey. The young stranger proved himself to be a delightful traveling companion and an expert in the art of camping. He knew all the dangers to be avoided, and when the pair were crossing the Euphrates river, he fought off a giant fish which attacked Tobias. Not merely that; he caught and killed the fish, whose well-grilled flesh was delicious, and whose liver, he said, had great value. Thanks to his new-found friend, Tobias found all obstacles smoothed in his journey. When evil spirits attacked him and tried to kill him, the liver of the fish his friend had killed protected him from them. At the end of the journey, the same friend collected his money for him while Tobias was getting married to a charming girl with whom he had fallen in love. Everything went splendidly.

Finally Tobias and his wife, accompanied by their good friend and Tobias' faithful dog, set their faces for home. As Tobias approached his native village he saw from afar his poor old blind father tottering forward to greet him. He hastened to embrace the old man while the dog went wild with joy at the reunion. Tobias had carefully preserved what was left of the liver of the strange fish that had attacked him when he was crossing the Euphrates and now, on the advice of his traveling companion, he anointed his father's eyes with it. Instantly, the old man's sight was restored.

We can well imagine the gratitude of father and son to their good friend! Tobias begged to be allowed to pay him in return for all his kindness. But, as he spoke, the young stranger was transformed into a shining being who declared, "I am an Angel of the Most High. Since you have always been faithful to Him, He sent me to help you in your need." And with this, he vanished. . . .

The story of the good Job, as preserved in the traditions of Israel, was an equally comforting one, for it too tells how in the end God brings consolation to those who have complete trust in Him.

One day, when all the angels of heaven were assembled at the throne of the Most High, they were joined by Satan, the prince of Evil. "Why do you come here?" the Lord asked him. To this Satan replied, "I have gone round about the earth and walked through it."

"Did you see my servant Job?" asked the Lord. "On all the earth there is no man like him, as full of faith, as upright, and avoiding evil."

"He deserves little credit for that," jeered the dark angel. "He is wealthy, happy, has a fine family and is rich in goods and livestock. But deprive him of what he has and we will soon see how faithful he is to You."

"Very well," said God, "I will do as you say and we will see what happens."

Forthwith, God allowed the devil to send one misfortune after another on the unfortunate Job. His great herds were stolen by robbers; his farm buildings were burned to the ground; his house was destroyed in a violent wind from the desert, and his children buried in the ruins. But Job never wavered in his faith. "The Lord gave, and the Lord has taken away. Blessed be the name of the Lord; His Will be done."

Wild with rage, Satan showered more misfortunes on Job and afflicted him with a grievous ulcer, so that his neighbors drove him away. He now had no roof over his head, and to avoid the chills of the night he had to camp on the dunghill on the outskirts of the village. His wife, who was inclined to nag, and his neighbors taunted him, saying, "What sins have you committed that God should persecute you so, this God in whom you believe? Better curse Him and die." To these jeers Job replied calmly and full of confidence, "If I

have sinned, may the Lord forgive me, and may my suffering pay for my sins. But I will not curse His Holy Name, nor will I give up my faith in Him."

At this, Satan had to admit himself beaten and gave up his persecution of God's faithful servant. Job, who was a truly saintly man, and who had in all his trials shown such perfect obedience to the Will of God, asked for no reward on earth. Nevertheless his All-powerful Master gave him fourteen thousand sheep, six thousand camels, a thousand pair of oxen and a thousand she-asses. He also blessed him with a fine family of seven sturdy boys and three lovely girls. Was it not to be hoped, therefore, that what God had done for Job He would do for His unhappy people when their sins had been sufficiently punished?

And now, sure enough, a rumor spread among the scattered group of exiles that a man had appeared who foretold that the end of their sufferings was at hand. This man was called Daniel, and the Bible and tradition tell us that he was a prophet who from his youth had shown himself to be a spokesman of God. He first revealed his mission as prophet when he played a remarkable part in a legal trial.

A young woman named Susanna had been charged with a very grave crime by two old men and was condemned to death on their evidence. Just as Susanna was being led to execution, God inspired the young Daniel to protest. "Hear me, people of Israel! This girl is innocent, do not put her to death, but give her a new trial." The execution party halted and asked Daniel what he had to say. "Susanna had been condemned on false evidence. These two old men are lying, for they hate the girl and seek to be revenged on her." Daniel so impressed his hearers that, young as he was, they entrusted him to investigate the matter. He interviewed the two old men separately, asking each of them, "Under what sort of tree did Susanna commit the crime with which you have charged her?" One replied, "Under a mastic tree." The other said, "Under a holm oak." Now these two trees are completely different in appearance and it was evident that the witnesses were telling lies. Susanna's innocence was proved, and it was her wicked accusers who were executed.

Throughout his life, Daniel always retained the great wisdom with which God had endowed him. In addition, no one was so ardent in his faith or so faithful to the commandments of the Lord. As a youth he had entered the service of the king of Babylon as a page, and had been brought up in the royal palace; but, for fear lest he should be served with meat and wines that had been offered to false idols, he ate only vegetables and drank nothing but water. This diet in no way affected his health, for he grew to be a sturdy, rosy-cheeked lad, as strong as any other boy of his age.

Among his many strange gifts not the least strange was his power of interpreting dreams. Like Joseph before Pharao—as you will remember—he was often called upon by the king to explain the meaning of dreams that had disturbed him.

One morning the king sent for Daniel and said to him, "I dreamed that I saw a great statue; its head was made of gold, its arms were silver, its legs were brass and its feet were made of iron and clay. Suddenly a stone fell from above on the statue and broke it into pieces. What does this mean?"

"It means, O King," replied Daniel, "that invaders from the mountains will destroy your kingdom, and that after it has fallen three other empires will be established which in their turn are also fated to disappear."

We know from history that Daniel's prophecy was true, for after the fall of the Babylonian empire came those of Persia, of Alexander of Macedon, and of Rome, which one after the other passed away. Like all the great Prophets, Daniel could see into the future, and in many passages of his book we find prophecies dealing with the very distant future, even with the coming of the Messias, who was not to be born for another five hundred years.

We can well imagine the influence enjoyed by the young prophet and the jealousies his power aroused. His enemies tried to ruin him many times. He was accused of being the enemy of the gods of Babylon, and they tried to force him to worship their idols. When Daniel refused, he was cast into a den of lions; but, by God's command, the beasts did him no injury, and crouched obediently at his feet as he prayed to the Lord God.

On another occasion his enemies attacked him through his dearest friends: three of his disciples were cast alive into a fiery furnace. You can imagine the surprise of the king's executioners when they heard coming from the furnace a song in praise of God. Looking in, they saw the three disciples unharmed in the midst of the flames. Terrified, the executioners ran away.

Such was the man who foretold the end of their trials to the people of Israel. It was not long before Daniel's prophecies were proved true. One night when Baltasar, the new king of Babylon, was feasting with his court, a mysterious hand appeared in the banquet hall like a trail of fire and traced on the wall just facing the king, the following words, "Mane, Thecel, Phares." The terrified Baltasar cried out, "I will give a purple mantle, a golden chain about his neck, and third place in my kingdom to whoever will translate these words for me."

Daniel appeared and told the king: "Mane, Thecel, Phares—which means, counted, weighed, divided! God has measured your reign and is about to finish it. You have been weighed in His balance and found wanting. Your kingdom will be divided between the Medes and the Persians."

That very night, the Persian army took Babylon by storm and Baltasar was killed.

XVI

Israel's Return to the Promised Land

WHO THEN were these Persians who broke the power of Babylon? They play such a large part in Bible history that you should know something about them—besides you will hear of them elsewhere in your school lessons. The Persians and their cousins, the Medes, were Aryans; that is, they came of the same stock as the Greeks, the Latins, and the Gauls from whom most of us are descended. They dwelt in the highlands to the east of Mesopotamia, in the region which they called "Aryana" that is, "the country of the Aryans." From this comes Iran, the modern name of Persia (see map on p. 106).

Starting off as simple shepherds and herdsmen, they had by the sixth century B.C. organized themselves into a powerful nation with a highly developed civilization. They were cultivated in the arts, and their cities of Pasargadae and Persepolis were filled with palaces, not as huge as those of Babylon, but elegant and beautiful, with slender columns and decorated ceilings. Their walls were adorned with brightly-colored bricks arranged to form real pictures; you may have seen photographs of the famous "frieze of archers." It is now in the Louvre Museum in Paris, and shows in enameled clay the soldiers of the Persian king's bodyguard in their splendid attire.

The Persian civilization was a humane one. They did not commit atrocities like the Assyrians, nor would they carry a whole people into exile as did Nabuchodonosor. Their religion differed greatly from that of the Hebrews, and was not of course equal to the latter which had been revealed by God Himself, but it contained much that was good. The Persians believed that the world was a battlefield between two major gods: the god of Good and the god of Evil, and that man's first duty on earth was to help the forces of Good to triumph over their abominable enemy.

So thought Cyrus, the Persian "King of Kings." He was a very great leader, and had already defeated Croesus, conquered Asia Minor, and reached the Mediterranean coast. He now turned his forces against Mesopotamia, at this time under the rule of a not very brilliant king. It is said that, in order to capture Babylon, a Persian general dammed the Euphrates river and diverted it from its course, thus enabling his soldiers to attack the city at a point where there were no defenses. At any rate, the year 539 B.C. saw the fulfilment of Isaias' prophecy of the fall of the capital. And now Cyrus became the most powerful emperor in the world.

One fine morning, envoys of the King of Kings (the title borne by the Persian sovereigns) appeared in the scattered villages of the Hebrew exiles to read the following decree:

"These are the orders of Cyrus! God, who has given all kingdoms into my hand, wishes that His Temple at Jerusalem in Judea be rebuilt. Let all His people know this. Let them return to their own country and there rebuild the House of God. It is my order that they receive help in money, clothing, and livestock, and that they be a free people once again."

What joy there was at this news, and how the Israelites cried out in gratitude to the generous conqueror of Babylon! Everything had happened exactly as the holy Prophets had foretold; Israel had atoned for her sins and God had pardoned His people. "When the Lord brought back the captivity of Sion, we became like men comforted. Then our mouth was filled with gladness, and our tongue with joy." So runs one of the Psalms in the Bible.

Once more the Israelites packed up, but this time their hearts were full of hope. What a wonderful thing it was to be free after half a century of slavery! Caravans were formed to bring the Israelites back to the Promised Land. For the most part, however, the people who returned were not those who had come into exile. A generation dies out in half a century, and it was the children or grandchildren of the deportees of 586 who prepared to return to Palestine. Nevertheless, these young people willingly forsook the life they had known on the banks of the Euphrates and launched themselves into the unknown, because God had ordered them to do so, and because love of their own country was their strongest feeling. What a splendid example of faith and of patriotism! From now on, the chosen people knew what it was its duty to do.

As the caravans wound their way along the desert tracks, the Israelites, keeping time to the beat of their camels' tread, sang this time a canticle of joy:

> The land that was desolate and impassable shall be glad, and the wilderness shall rejoice, and shall flourish like the lily.
>
> It shall bud forth and blossom, and shall rejoice with joy and praise: the glory of Libanus is given to it: the beauty of Carmel and Saron, they shall see the glory of the Lord, and the beauty of God.

It must be admitted that not all of the Israelites returned to Palestine. This is easily understood when we realize that many of the exiles had built up businesses in Mesopotamia which they could not sell, and that others had aged and sick relatives who could not undertake the journey. Men are never over-anxious to undertake a great act of heroism when it means the sacrifice of all their wealth and comforts. So we find that Israelite colonies remained in the Persian empire, just as today in every American and European country we find Jewish communities mixed with the rest of the population. Some of those Israelites who remained in Mesopotamia became bankers, others public-works inspectors, or tax collectors; in other words, they served the Persian kings as officials.

Being highly intelligent, many of the Israelites rose to positions of great power and wealth, and at times their success provoked much jealousy. As an example of this, the Bible tells us the story of Esther.

The king of Persia at this time was Assuerus, grandson of the great Cyrus. You probably know this name, indeed you should, for it is well known both in history and in literature. The great French poet Racine, who wrote a poem on Esther, makes much mention of Assuerus, and in history he was none other than the king whom the Greeks called Xerxes, who was their enemy and whom they defeated at the famous naval battle of Salamis.

Assuerus, then, was the ruler of Persia. Among his many wives was a young and beautiful Israelite called Esther, who was the niece of the holy old man Mardochai. Due to her beauty and to her wit, Esther had great influence over her husband, and had placed many of her people in court positions. Through her, her friends and relatives played an important part in the government of the country, and this was the cause of much jealousy.

The king's principal minister, Aman, was particularly angry at the position held by the Israelites. An incident occurred that made him angrier still: Mardochai learned by chance of a plot by a group of rebels against the king and warned Assuerus of his danger. Aman decided to rid himself of such rivals and succeeded in getting permission for a general massacre of all Israelites in the empire on a certain day, under the pretext that they were plotting against the king and were disloyal to the laws of Persia.

The protection of God, however, was still over His people. Mardochai learned of the dreadful plan. He informed his niece and commanded her, in God's name, to seek out the king and to implore him not to sign the decree for the massacre. Putting on her best attire, Esther presented herself before the king and, kneeling at his feet, explained matters to him and implored his help.

It happened that at the moment when Esther approached him, Assuerus was reading the day-to-day reports of the events of his

reign, and he had just reached the report of how Mardochai had saved his life by warning him of the rebel plot. He was angry that Aman should plot the destruction of this people which had been so loyal to him. He sent at once for the principal minister. "What should I do?" he asked him, "to honor a man for great loyalty?" Thinking that the man referred to was himself and that the king was planning some splendid reward for him, Aman replied, "Sire, I would suggest that such a man be clothed in one of your own garments, and be set on a horse from the royal stables; that a jewel be placed on his headdress, and thus equipped that he be led in procession through all the streets of your capital."

"An excellent idea," replied Assuerus. "I now order you personally to see that these honors are paid to Mardochai, the holy elder of Israel."

And there is the story of how Aman lost his position as principal minister and how Mardochai won it.

Let us now return to the Israelites who had made their way back to the Promised Land. As they were not very numerous, they settled around Jerusalem in the region known as Judea (see map on front endpaper). Now an inhabitant of Judea was known in Latin as "Judaeus," which is translated into English as "Jew." It was from the period of their return from Babylon that the Israelite people began to be known as Jews.

It was by no means easy for the Jews to settle again in Palestine. The last fifty years had seen many changes in the country. Some of the towns and villages that had been destroyed by the Babylonians were still horrible masses of rubble. The fields were choked with weeds and briars. Moreover, much of the ownerless land had been occupied by the desert Bedouins who showed no inclination to give it up. It was a very difficult situation. But since God in His mercy had led the Israelites back to the land of their fathers, who among them would let himself be overcome by obstacles, or refrain from making every possible effort to restore the country after its terrible disaster?

So, forthwith, everyone set to work. Of course, the first task was the reconstruction of the Temple, as a mark of His people's gratitude to the Lord God. They had not, alas, the mighty resources of the great King Solomon, his gold, his precious woods, his Tyrian architects, or his thousands of skilled craftsmen. Still everyone worked with a will under the leadership of two prophets, Aggeus and Zacharias, whose burning words kept up the people's enthusiasm and spurred them on to greater effort. "Go up to the mountains and bring wood," ordered Aggeus. "Work to build the Temple if you wish to glorify and please God."

Finally, after four and a half years, the new Temple was completed. It was a much smaller and more modest building than that erected by Solomon. Instead of ten golden hanging lamps there was only one, and there was no sweet-scented sandalwood to line the walls of the sanctuary. It was a shrine erected by a poor people who had known much suffering. But what did it matter? What pleases God is not a display of wealth, but goodwill among men and the sincere love of faithful hearts.

When the Temple had been completed, the people's next task was the fortification of the Holy City, for Jerusalem was threatened by many enemies, and in particular by the Samaritans. Samaria was now populated by a mixture of peoples planted there by the Assyrians, people who called themselves Hebrews but who, in fact, were half pagan and who hated the followers of the True God.

The honor of rebuilding the walls of Jerusalem fell upon Nehemias. Everything went well from the moment he took charge. He mobilized every Jew capable of manual labor, and to make sure their enemies would not take them by surprise, each worker was ordered to keep his sword by his side at all times. The fortifications were completed after fifty-two days of frenzied labor. This was in the year 445 B.C.

While these events were taking place in Judea, let us see what was happening in the rest of the ancient world. In Greece, the Athenians had won a brilliant victory over the Persians. Under the leadership of Pericles, they had reached the peak of their civilization and had built their famous temple, the Parthenon. In Italy, Rome had become a Republic and had proclaimed its celebrated "Law of Twelve Tables." For the rest, our European ancestors in Gaul and elsewhere, consisting mainly of fierce and warlike tribes, were roaming far and wide engaged in plundering expeditions.

The Bible tells us little of the centuries which followed. Israel was no longer an independent kingdom but a simple province in the vast Persian empire which reached from Egypt, which also had been conquered, to the frontiers of India. The Persian empire was magnificently organized, and the rule of law and order prevailed everywhere in it. From his capital city where he dwelled in great luxury, dressed in jewel-embroidered garments and wearing his golden tiara, the emperor kept strict watch over his thirty provinces. His vast territories were criss-crossed by splendid roads where, at regular intervals, couriers, or imperial messengers, found fresh horses awaiting them so that they could gallop on their way carrying the emperor's orders with incredible speed. And everywhere the royal inspectors, known as "the eyes and ears of the Master," saw to it that the emperor's wishes were obeyed.

From now on Israel was not an independent state. The Persian kings were wise rulers who did not try to force their countless subjects into ways they did not want, and God's people were allowed to practice their religion in peace. The king was content to govern though his "satrap," who was a sort of provincial governor or prefect. So long as order prevailed, the different peoples in the empire could do very much as they liked.

So it was that Israel with its modest territory became but a religious community, the Jewish community. The inheritors of the past glories of Israel now realized that for them only one thing mattered: their faith, their religion, their devotion to the Eternal God. They eagerly studied all that their ancient traditions had to tell them about their great forefathers, Abraham, Moses, David, Solomon, and the Prophets.

It was then that, to help his people, a man inspired by God, called Esdras, decided to gather together all the oral and written traditions that had been such an inspiration to Israel in her days of darkness. Esdras did much to prepare the official list of texts which were finally approved. Thus the Bible as we read it today has been in existence since the middle of the fifth century B.C., that is, for about 2,400 years.

XVII

The Beauty and Wisdom of the Bible

SINCE THE BIBLE is Holy Scripture, it is important for us to know how Esdras and those who worked with him selected the sacred texts. Which, among all the traditional stories that had been handed down from generation to generation by word of mouth in Israel, were selected, and why were these particular texts chosen? Only those were retained which it was certain were inspired by God. This means that those who uttered them did so under a direct impulse from heaven, an inspiration that saved them from human error and gave them a knowledge not possessed by ordinary men. For example, we know that Moses and the Prophets spoke in the Name of God and, as it were, at His dictation. This is the reason the Biblical texts are so beautiful, and why they still teach us the Law of God.

When Esdras and his helpers had completed their work, the Bible consisted of some forty books. A little later, more books were added, making a total of forty-six books which compose that part of the Bible which we call the Old Testament today. The meaning of the words "Old Testament" is easy to understand: the Latin word *testamentum* simply means testimony or evidence—the Bible is the testimony of God. You may ask, "Why Old? Is there then a New Testament?" There is indeed, for after the people of Israel had said all they had to say, Jesus Christ, Our Lord, came to earth to teach mankind the whole truth with the authority of His Divine Word. God sent amongst us His only Divine Son who became a man similar to ourselves. The New Testament is the testimony of all that Jesus Christ did and taught during His life on earth; the Old Testament is the testimony of Israel.

The Old Testament's forty-six books vary greatly in character. At the beginning we find the story of the creation of the world and of man; of the fall of Adam, and so on to the time of the Tower of Babel. Next come a series of books dealing with the important events that took place and the great figures which appeared in the history of Israel down the centuries. Then we come to a lengthy account of the sayings and deeds of the Prophets of Israel. Finally, there are still other books composed of poetry and of meditation on the great problems of life, and these last are not by any means the least important or the least beautiful.

You may perhaps say to yourself, "What we have read up till now deals mainly with battles, wars, and all sorts of violence!" You are quite right, of course, and the reason is that the people of Israel, who were the sole believers in the True God, were in all their long history constantly being attacked by enemies, so that their story naturally has many warlike chapters. You must also understand that all the texts of the Bible have a religious meaning; they are not told merely as stories but because they teach faith and hope in God and the necessity of obedience to Him.

Another thing you must have noticed is the gift of poetry possessed by the people of Israel, although they lived under arms all the time. You must have been thrilled by the beauty of the Psalms of David and by the songs sung by Israel in the desert; songs of sadness as they left their home, songs of happiness as they returned, but both of them wondrously beautiful.

The finest of Jewish poetry is, in truth, religious. It is above all contained in the one hundred and fifty Psalms in which the people of Israel unceasingly sing the glory of God and thank Him for His goodness.

> For who is God but the Lord? or
> Who is God but our God?
> God who hath girt me with strength;
> and made my way blameless.

Who hath made my feet like the feet of harts: and who setteth me upon high places.

Who teacheth my hands to war: and thou hast made my arms like a brazen bow.

Or again:

Thou hast visited the earth, and hast plentifully watered it; thou hast many ways enriched it.

The river of God is filled with water . . .

Thou shalt bless the crown of the year of thy goodness: and thy fields shall be filled with plenty.

The beautiful places of the wilderness shall grow fat: and the hills shall be girded about with joy,

> The rams of the flock are clothed,
> and the vales shall abound with corn:
> they shall shout, yea they shall sing a
> hymn.

Would it be possible to find more glowing words to express the gratitude that man should feel toward his Creator, the Master of all the things by which we live?

Not merely in these great religious hymns, but in other places in the Bible we find many passages of pure poetry, describing for example some aspect of the Holy Land. I would like to give you a few quotations so that you can appreciate their beauty. Listen, for example, to the picture the Bible gives us of springtime in Palestine:

> For winter is now past, the rain is over and gone.
>
> The flowers have appeared in our land, the time of pruning is come: the voice of the turtle is heard in our land:
>
> The fig tree hath put forth her green figs: the vines in flower yield their sweet smell.

Is not this poetry at its best?

And here are some comparisons found by a Biblical poet to describe a young woman's beauty:

> My spouse is a garden enclosed, a garden enclosed, a fountain sealed up.
>
> Thy plants are a paradise of pomegranates with the fruit of the orchard. Cypress with spikenard.
>
> Spikenard and saffron, sweet cane and cinnamon, with all the trees of Libanus, myrrh and aloes with all the chief perfumes.
>
> The fountain of gardens: the well of living waters, which run with a strong stream from Libanus.

> Arise, O north wind, and come, O
> south wind, blow through my garden,
> and let the aromatical spices thereof flow.

When you read this poem, do you not feel yourself transported on a summer's day to a shady garden filled with the tinkle of falling waters and heavy with the scent of flowers?

The two quotations which you have just read both come from the loveliest of all the books of poetry in the Bible, the Canticle of Canticles. Here is the delightful story that is told in this book.

Out in the desert, where the nomads dwelt in their black tents, there was a beautiful young girl who spent her time tending her flocks of goats and sheep. The king himself, who noticed her one day as he was passing, thought her so lovely that he married her and took her with him to his city. There, safe in the love of the all-powerful king, she was completely happy. She wanted for nothing and the king showered precious gifts on her: necklaces of coral, bracelets of gold, and the most costly of perfumes.

Careless in her good fortune, the young woman drew away from him who loved her. She ceased to be true to him, whereupon he too, naturally enough, withdrew from her. Now indeed the young woman was desolate for she thought that through her wickedness she had lost the love of her husband. One night therefore she arose and went to seek the one who had once loved her. She searched everywhere throughout the city, asking the watchmen, "Have you seen him whom my heart loves?" She was in despair at not finding him. Finally she sought him in the desert where, as he still truly loved her, he allowed her to join him. He forgave her and together they returned to the royal palace to renew their former happiness.

As you can guess, this love story did not find its place in the Bible merely because it was a charming tale and one that gave a delightful picture of the Palestine countryside. It was much more than this for, like many of the Bible texts, it had a hidden, or what we call a symbolic, meaning.

In it, the young woman represents the people of Israel and the king represents God. When Israel was wandering in the desert her people were chosen by God, who overwhelmed them with favors, giving them a beautiful country and a splendid city. But, like the young woman, the people were fickle and did not remain true to the Lord. So it was that He withdrew His favor and all sorts of misfortunes and unhappiness overtook them, as we have seen. But the end of the story contains the promise that God will forgive His chosen people. Once again Israel will enjoy His favor, and in the people's love for God they will regain their former happiness and prosperity.

You have seen how splendid is the poetry of the Bible, but you should also observe the great number of passages in the Holy Book which contain astonishing sentences over which we may well ponder. For the most part, these sentences are short and very simple, but they contain so much wisdom that even today we should think deeply about them. They are to be found scattered everywhere throughout the pages of the Bible; in the Book of Psalms as in the Book of Prophets; indeed two whole books, Ecclesiastes and Proverbs, consist entirely of them.

Let us open this last book at random and see what we find:

"A wise son heareth his father: but he that is a scorner, heareth not when he is reproved." Is not that absolutely true? "Go to the ant, O sluggard, and consider her ways and learn wisdom." Is not this also quite true? Here is one sentence the truth of which you can prove for yourself every day: "The innocent believeth every word: the discreet man considereth his steps." Here is yet another saying which warns you to distrust people who try to flatter you: "The dissembler with his mouth deceiveth his friend." Is not all this well said and perfectly expressed?

Besides, many of these sayings have passed into all languages as maxims, and many of those with which we are most familiar come straight from the pages of the Bible:

"Hope that is deferred afflicteth the soul."

"A mild answer breaketh wrath."

"A glad heart maketh a cheerful countenance."

"Get wisdom because it is better than gold."

All these sayings and others equally well known, come from the Book of Proverbs, and it is from the Book of Ecclesiastes that come two other famous phrases: "Vanity of vanities" (which means that it is wrong for man to pride himself on earthly success, since one day he will die), and, "Nothing new under the sun" (which means that most of the things men believe to be new were already known to the ancients). You can see from this the great influence of the old Biblical texts and the great wisdom of those who first wrote them down.

Of course, the most beautiful thing about the Bible is the religion which inspires it. The essential character of all Holy Writ is the yearning toward God that is to be found on every page, and which transforms all its accounts of war, its travel stories, its poems, and its meditations into one great prayer. It was this yearning for God that gave Israel her grandeur, for from the time of Abraham she never ceased to love Him, to think about Him and, despite all her sins, to labor for His glory.

A remarkable and admirable thing about the people of Israel is the fact that as the centuries passed they understood their religion better and better and strove to perfect it. In the time of Abraham the people's faith was a simple one; all that was needed was to believe in God. With Moses came the Ten Commandments of God, a more complete and detailed rule of faith. At the time of the Prophets, the Hebrew religion came to include many fine and noble teachings which were the forerunners of Christianity. In fact, it came to the people of Israel as it does to a child: when you were a tiny child you understood very little, but gradually as you grew you were taught more and more. When you are fully grown, you will understand many more things that now are too difficult for you. Your teachers, your parents and your priests, as they take you through your catechism, will have much to tell you. The Prophets, who were inspired by God, were to some extent the teachers of Israel.

By the time that the Bible had been set down in writing, that is, in the final centuries of the history of Israel, the Jewish religion had become a magnificent institution. Then, as always, its first and sole object was to serve and glorify God, the True God, the Only God, as the people's ancestors had always done. Men knew that He was the Eternal God, the All-Powerful God, the Mighty God, whose Name could only be uttered on bended knees. But they also knew that the same God was, above all, the God of goodness and of justice, the God who punished the sins of man but who afterward pardoned them and who extended His mercy to the weak, the unhappy and the oppressed.

What then must man do? He must adore God alone, but he must also obey the laws which God has made. Disobedience to God is a sin, and in sin man's mind is in a state of misery and suffering. The just man is happy and enjoys God's protection. What must we do to become just? To be just we must first of all avoid the sins forbidden by the Commandments: we must not steal, or tell lies, or commit murder. But this is not enough. We must do good to our fellow man, and treat our neighbor as we hope God will treat us. In the Bible we read this fine rule of conduct, "If thy enemy be hungry, give him to eat: if he be thirsty, give him water to drink." In the Bible also are some very humane rules; for instance, the one that commands the harvester to leave behind stray stalks of grain so that the poor can glean them (do you remember the story of Ruth?) or the one that says that if a man takes another's coat as pledge for a loan, he must return it to him at night for warmth.

And how, according to the Hebrews, did God reward or punish man for his conduct? In the very early days and even down to the time of the Exile, it was believed that the Lord rewarded his faithful servants with great riches and earthly happiness; but little by little people realized that this was not always God's plan. Were there not many good men, firm believers, who lived in poverty and distress? So at last people understand that God inflicted trials on such people for their own good, to detach them from earthly things, and to prepare them for other rewards. Finally, came realization of the truth: after death God judges all men according to their actions, punishing the wicked and rewarding the good with eternal happiness.

So you see how it was that in two thousand years of meditation and prayer and inspired by God, Israel discovered a great many truths. Not all, however, for before the whole truth could be revealed the world would have to advance a further stage in order to receive the words of final authority—those of Our Lord Jesus Christ.

XVIII

Life in Israel Before the Coming of Christ

LET US NOW TRY to picture for ourselves the sort of life led by a believing Jew in the final years before our era, just before the birth of Jesus. Let us take as our example neither a priest nor a scholar but a simple man of the people, say, a working carpenter. We will call him Joseph, a common enough name. First of all we will try to understand the part played by religion in his daily life.

When he rises in the morning he is scarcely out of bed when he turns toward the Temple and recites the following prayer: "Hear, O Israel, our God is the True God, the Only God." He will repeat the same prayer in the evening when the setting sun is shedding its last rays upon the mountain slopes before it plunges into the sea. This, however, is not the only prayer that Joseph will recite. During the day, he will chant the eighteen long blessings in which God is thanked for all His goodness. Every action of his will be preceded by prayer; he will pray before leaving his house, before he eats or drinks, when he meets a friend. . . . He will often utter the joyous cry that is still heard in our churches: "Alleluia! Glory to God in the highest!"

You see therefore that Joseph can do nothing without thinking of his God and of his religion. This is not surprising, for Joseph well knows who saved Israel when she was surrounded by enemies who wished her death. Who but the Almighty? And what was it that enabled his people during their exile in Babylon to preserve their national traditions and so to survive the trial? Was it not the Bible, the sacred inspired text of Israel? So it is no wonder that the people study so earnestly the Book of God's Law. When Joseph was quite small he was taught how to read with the help of the Bible, spelling out his first letters from its sacred pages. These pages were written in Hebrew (just as the prayers of the Mass are written in Latin), a language which was no longer spoken in Judea. People there now spoke Aramaic (another Semitic tongue widely used in the East), but there was not a single Jew who did not know enough Hebrew to understand the principal prayers and to enable him when he went to the Temple to sing the responses to the Psalms.

But Joseph has by no means performed all his religious duties when he has said some prayers. On the contrary. The Jewish Law is wonderfully precise and imposes all sorts of minor obligations on its pious followers. Is Joseph going to buy meat in the market? He must make sure that the animal has been killed according to the Jewish ritual, and not as the pagans kill their beasts. Does he wish to sell vegetables from his garden? He cannot do so until he has offered the tenth part to the Temple: one-tenth of all produce of the fields is due to the Temple, and it is a grave sin to eat a vegetable on which this levy has not been paid.

If the day happens to be Saturday, the regulations are still more severe, for Saturday is the Sabbath, the day of rest which God ordered Moses to observe. From morning to night all work is strictly forbidden, and Joseph may not even write a letter or deliver a package. The entire day must be devoted to meditation and prayer, and a heavy punishment awaits anyone who violates the Sabbath rules.

But suppose today is not merely the Sabbath; it is also a solemn feast. Let us follow Joseph as he plods up and down the hilly streets of Jerusalem and find out where he and all the other people who are traveling in the same direction are going. To the Temple, of course, to the thrice-sacred place where God Himself is present, though invisible. The eager crowd is hurrying now, so let us follow Joseph into the Temple and look about us.

We find ourselves in the first courtyard, which all true mem-

COURT OF PEOPLE
ALTAR
COURT OF PRIESTS
BRAZEN SEA
COURT OF WOMEN
COURT OF PEOPLE
OUTER COURT

bers of the Jewish race have the right to enter. It is a huge terraced enclosure surrounding the entrances to the Temple proper, and is always a scene of almost incredible activity. What are these open-air booths under the galleries where men are weighing pieces of silver on delicate scales? These are the money changers, for no one may offer a Greek "drachma" or a Persian "daric" to the Temple; only Jewish coins, actually minted in the Temple itself, will be accepted. And, in a corner of the courtyard, what are these animals whose bleating and bellowing can be heard above the voices of the dealers? These are the animals for sacrifice, and if Joseph wishes to offer up a lamb or a dove to the Lord (he would not be able to afford a bull) he will find one here.

Suddenly the air is filled with a piercing noise and a movement ripples through the crowd. The High Priest! The silver trumpets proclaim his approach, and their strident blare will be repeated three times. The final long blast will tell the people that the dignitary has entered the sanctuary. Joseph has hastened to cover his head with a piece of white cloth called the *talith,* which must be worn by all taking part in the Temple ceremonies, and to fasten to his wrists and forehead little boxes which contain verses from the Bible.

Now the ceremony is about to commence. Joseph must follow it from afar for, not being a Levite, he cannot enter the second courtyard, the priests' enclosure. It is here that stands the huge font used for ritual ablutions (in other days it was called the Sea of Brass and rested on four groups of three bronze oxen). Here also is the altar where beasts are sacrificed and where burns a perpetual fire.

Mixing in the crowd Joseph's gaze follows the procession as it moves slowly forward. What a majestic figure is the High Priest, wearing his tall miter, clad in a robe of dark purple bound with a broad silken belt, and wearing on his breast his pectoral, a piece of material studded with precious stones! The good folk gaze with awe at him and think to themselves, "How fortunate is this man who alone has the right to enter the most secret shrine of the Temple, the shrine where dwells our unseen God!"

Followed by a long procession, the High Priest reaches the door of the sanctuary. He passes around the tall column which appears to be guarding the entrance, passes between two columns of bronze, and crosses the threshold of the Holy Place. It is here that each day a priest chosen by lot comes to burn incense on the altar; it is here that blaze the flames of the seven-branched candlestick; it is here that is offered to the Lord the bread of sacrifice or the "loaves of proposition."

If it is a really solemn occasion, the white curtain embroidered in purple and gold, which is draped across the entrance to the Holy of Holies, is drawn aside and the High Priest enters, while the congregation remain motionless in silent prayer. In Solomon's time the Holy of Holies contained the Ark of the Covenant, but in the disaster of 586 B.C. the Babylonians destroyed it, and it was never restored. As, of course, idols are forbidden, the sanctuary is empty; there silence alone keeps its eternal vigil. . . .

Festivals of the kind we have described take place many times during the year. Each has its own character and significance, for each commemorates some ancient tradition of Israel, and the rituals have been handed down from generation to generation.

The most important feast of the year is the Passover, celebrated in the spring after the first new moon in April. For two weeks bonfires blaze merrily on every hill and mountain, so that it seems as if the very ground itself is offering prayer to God. As the evening of the Paschal feast approaches, let us see what our friend Joseph is going to do. He has already bought a lamb which will be sacrificed at nightfall on the eve of the feast. Later Joseph will eat the lamb as part of a very interesting ceremony for, in fact, the Paschal Lamb commemorates the lamb that Joseph's ancestors sacrificed in Egypt by Moses' command long, long ago as they prepared for their hurried flight from Pharao. Therefore, it was the law that the people must dress in traveling clothes, carry a staff in one hand, and stand upright to eat the lamb as though once again they were preparing to flee into the desert.

The actual sojourn in the desert is commemorated by another feast, this time a very gay and happy one. It takes place in the autumn, when the grapes and other crops have been gathered and the farmers' yearly round of work is coming to its close. It is called the Feast of Tents or of Tabernacles, and lasts for nine days during which everyone must leave his home and live for a short while the nomad life once led by the people of Israel. All round the city and in the squares and open places in it, the people have erected huts of foliage in which they live during the entire period of the celebrations. As the autumn climate of Palestine is perfect, it is a glorious outing for everybody. Each evening the High Priest and the Levites will march in procession to the finest well in Jerusalem and draw water from it. This they bring back to the Temple as an offering to God. As you will remember, water was scarce and difficult to find in the desert, and the people owed thanks to God for not letting them die of thirst.

There were many other feasts, such as the Feast of Weeks, which commemorated God's great gift to His people on Mount Sinai, when He made known His will to them and gave them His Ten Commandments. It is this feast which developed with an even more beautiful significance into our Pentecost.

Then there was another feast of a very different kind, when only Psalms of lamentation were sung, and where the congregation appeared weeping and wearing mourning garments. This was called the Feast of Expiation. On that day Israel remembered its many sins and begged God to forgive them. The ugliest and smelliest old buck goat that could be found was brought before the High Priest, who pronounced words over him which meant, "I hereby lay upon you all the sins of our people." After this the buck goat was driven out into the desert where it was believed the devil would seize him.

You may well say that all that I have told you concerns Jerusalem only, which barely held one-tenth of the population of Palestine. How about the rest of the country? Were there not other temples besides that of Sion? No, there was only one Temple for the One True God, and the Samaritans who had set up a sanctuary—as a rival to that of the Holy City—were looked upon as traitors and heretics.

How then did the people in the provinces worship? For all the great festivals, and especially for the Passover, thousands upon thousands of them journeyed to Jerusalem. The streets of the capital and the courtyard of the Temple were packed with these pilgrims who, when the feast was over, wended their way home happily, singing Psalms of rejoicing as they went.

Apart from these festivals, the people, both in Jerusalem and in the provinces, had their meeting halls which they called synagogues, a name given by Jews to their places of worship to this day. Neither ceremonies nor sacrifices took place in the synagogue, but scholars who had made a special study of the Bible, scribes or doctors of the Law they were called, explained them to the people. Here also the children came for their lessons for, as we have seen, the education of Jewish children consisted mainly of readings from the Scriptures.

When you try to picture for yourself the childhood of Jesus think of Him, at your own age, sitting on a bench in the synagogue of Nazareth and with his school companions reciting aloud the verses of the Bible which He, of course, understood instantly at the first reading.

This then was how the Jews lived. Following their return from Babylon, they had withdrawn themselves into a separate community, as do people who have suffered a great deal. Israel now had only one occupation, one object in life: to serve God, to study His teaching, and to be utterly faithful to Him. Israel had traveled far from the visions of earthly glory which she cherished in the time of

Solomon. She no longer sought power and splendor, but the mercy and the love of God.

As Israel was no longer an independent state, there was no king. The country was administered by an official of the ruling power in Palestine: first a Persian, then a Greek, then a Roman; it mattered little. The Jewish community thought much more of its religion than it did of political liberty, and its real leaders were its religious superiors: the High Priest and the seventy members of a sort of tribunal that was called the Sanhedrin.

The strength of Israel in those last centuries before our era lay in her heroic devotion to the true religion, a devotion that overcame all trials. There were now isolated groups of Jews everywhere throughout the civilized world—in Egypt, Greece and Rome. But scattered as they were, they considered themselves as one in race and soul with their community, for each day they turned toward Jerusalem in prayer, each year they sent their offering of gold to the Temple, and once at least in their lives they made their pilgrimage to the courts of Sion.

Thus the pagans could try in vain to impose their idol worship on this small people of the Lord. Israel stubbornly refused to accept any foreign influence, and to the very last and at the price of her own blood she would steadfastly proclaim her faith in the One True God.

XIX

The Jews' Heroic Stand Against Paganism

"RESIST, O ISRAEL, resist until death! Never, never will we accept false gods or bow down to the idols of Persia, Greece and Rome. We are the servants of the One True God: Him only do we know and His laws only will we obey."

Unyielding and passionate, this was the repeated cry of the people of Israel during the five centuries that elapsed between their return from the Babylonian captivity and the birth of Christ. How splendid is the resolve of this weak people, no longer an independent nation but one which at least has preserved the most precious liberty of all—the right to follow its conscience and to practice the religion in which it so fervently believes.

To help you to understand fully what took place in Palestine at this time we must refresh our memory of past history and then see what was going on in the rest of the world.

We had left Cyrus at the head of the Persian empire. When he died he was succeeded by his son Cambyses who continued his father's career of conquest by annexing Egypt, a very attractive prize indeed. Cambyses, however, lost his reason, and squandered his armies on impossible ventures so that eventually he faced rebellion within the empire. His cousin Darius I, who succeeded him, was an energetic man who restored order throughout his vast domains, but he made one mistake for which he had to pay dearly.

Facing his ports on the coast of Asia Minor was Greece, where had been established and now flourished that wonderful small nation which had given the world its greatest thinkers and artists. The Greeks were not a numerous people, and their chief cities, even Athens itself, were little more than villages. Darius despised them and thought that he could overthrow them with a turn of his wrist. But we all know what happened. The famous Median Wars took place, in the course of which the huge forces of the Medes and Persians were completely overthrown by the bravery of the Greeks, and in particular of the Athenians. At Marathon, in the year 490 B.C., the Greek "hoplites," or foot soldiers, threw the army of the King of Kings into the sea, and at Salamis in 480 their "triremes," or warships, sank his fleets.

Persia never recovered from this blow and now began to decline. It had never been easy to govern this immense empire, where thirty different languages were spoken. The powers of the kings were beginning to wane. And, now, to their great misfortune, they suddenly found themselves confronted by one of the greatest military leaders the world has even known, a young man only twenty years old who, having brought about the unity of Greece, now advanced to the attack on Asia. His name was Alexander of Macedon. Alexander was handsome as a god, brave and tireless, and he broke and captured the Persian empire in two years. He ruled the land from the Nile to the Euphrates and even penetrated as far as India. At the height of his fame, he died at the early age of thirty-two. This was in 323 B.C.

So it was that Palestine passed from the possession of Persia to that of Alexander; then, after the latter's dazzling career was over and his territories were being divided among his generals, Israel found herself a bone of contention between the new rulers of Egypt and of Asia Minor, both of them Greeks, of course. The Jews cared little about the change of masters, provided always that their rulers did not attempt to introduce their false gods into Chanaan.

Alexander had no more desire than had his Persian predecessors to persecute the faith of Israel. Indeed there is a Jewish tradition that the young conqueror, when passing through Jerusalem on his way to Egypt, was so delighted by the honors paid to him by the

High Priest that he not merely promised to see to it that God's laws were respected but himself actually made sacrifice to the Lord.

As time passed, however, the position changed for the worse. Several of Alexander's successors to the throne of Greece tried to introduce their own pagan cult into the Jewish community. Worse still, it must be admitted that there were some Jews who, in their admiration for the culture, intelligence and high standard of living of the Greeks, fell under their pagan influence. These were the dangers that faced the true servants of God, and in the centuries that followed they fought ceaselessly against the foreign enemy and his supporters within their gates.

Tradition has it that God Himself took part in the struggle and intervened on behalf of His people. Once, when the Greek king Seleucus had sent his envoy Heliodorus to despoil the Temple of its sacred treasure, a terrible horseman appeared and fell upon the thief. He was soon followed by two others and they beat Heliodorus so severely that he had to flee in great distress. The people had no doubt that the horsemen who inflicted this punishment were angels sent by God.

Things became worse still when a certain Antiochus IV, called by his subjects "the Illustrious," became ruler of Asia Minor. He appeared before Jerusalem with a mighty army, desecrated the Temple, and pillaged it of everything worth stealing. Thousands of faithful Jews were slaughtered. The walls, the cherished walls of Nehemias, were destroyed, and, like a dagger in the bosom of the Holy City, the king built a citadel overlooking the Temple in which he placed a garrison of soldiers. From now on, there was open religious persecution in all its horror: the Holy of Holies was profaned by an image of Zeus, the principal god of Greece; the reading of the Bible was forbidden; the observance of the Sabbath and of the Jewish festivals was forbidden.

These events which took place in 167 B.C. seemed to sound the death knell of Israel. Even the High Priests themselves abandoned the worship of the True God and became pagans!

But in all this misfortune there is a lesson to be learned which we should remember, for it has been proved true in many other places besides Palestine. The lesson is that a nation can only die when it has lost the will to survive and its respect for its glorious traditions. While some rich and powerful personages became traitors, the mass of the Jewish people remained faithful and continued to resist the onrush of paganism.

There were many acts of heroic resistance. There were many men and women who gave up everything—their houses, their lands, their property—and fled into the desert rather than accept paganism. Jewish history still tells the story of the martyrdom of a holy old man, Eleazar, who, when the pagans tried to make him eat meat that was forbidden by Jewish law, spat it out, knowing well that to do so would cost him torture. There is another pitiful story of a mother who saw her seven sons tortured before her eyes, but who to the very end urged them to face death rather than be untrue to God.

Finally, what we would call their underground resistance movement found leaders. These were the Machabees, an entire family of heroes—father, sons, nephews, and cousins—all equally brave and determined in their struggle against the infidel. The traitorous Jews who collaborated with the Greeks were hunted down. The garrisons planted by Antiochus had to beat a retreat. It was the last page in the glorious story of Israel.

The outstanding hero of this critical period was Judas Machabeus who, the Bible tells us, was as terrible in battle as "a lion roaring for his prey." The Greek governor was killed, and four armies sent to his relief were defeated one after the other. In the end, Antiochus had to restore religious liberty to the Jews, and Judas Machabeus, returning in triumph to Jerusalem, tore down the heathen idol which the Greeks had erected in the Temple, and reestablished the worship of the Lord.

The Machabean wars provide a splendid interlude of courage and faith in Jewish history. One of the most famous personages of

this time was Eleazar Machabeus. When in the midst of a battle he saw a richly adorned elephant which, he believed carried the enemy commander, he slipped under the animal to rip him open, and he was killed when the great beast collapsed on top of him.

The last of the great Machabees was John Hircanus who, between the years 134 and 104 B.C., won for them such power and glory that he reminded the people of Israel of the time of Solomon. He surrounded himself with regal pomp, reunited the three provinces of Palestine under his authority, recalled Galilee to the worship of the Lord, and defied the Greeks to interfere with him. He was the last really great figure in Bible history. We must now admit that after his death there came about a period of decadence and decline.

Now let us turn our eyes to another part of the world, to the city of Rome in Italy, where great events are about to take place. You may remember the hamlet founded in the marshes of the Tiber by

Romulus in the eighth century B.C., just at the time when the Assyrians were overthrowing Samaria. How this little town had grown since then! By the fifth century B.C., when Nehemias was rebuilding the walls of Jerusalem, Rome had become master of all Italy. She now faced her great rival Carthage, the wealthy Phenician colony on the African coast which stood near the site of present-day Tunis. By the end of these wars, called the Punic Wars, Rome had destroyed Carthage. But it had been no easy struggle, and several times it had been touch-and-go for the Romans. Once, for example, during the Second Punic War (218–201 B.C.), the Carthaginian general Hannibal had crossed the Alps with his elephants and had invaded Italy.

The Romans now turned to the East. They had made a Roman province of Greece in the same year (146 B.C.), they had at last captured Carthage, and completely destroyed it. They made their way into Asia, also occupied Egypt. Soon Palestine was to echo with the tramp of the tireless Roman legions, to see their rounded helmets and long javelins.

It was the descendants of the Machabees who had summoned them there. Unworthy successors to the heroes of the Jewish resistance, these Jewish kings spent their time in bloody quarrels and in subduing by terror the revolts of their own subjects. Did not one of them crucify on the terrace of his palace six hundred rebels whom he had captured, and did he not have the further cruelty to massacre the wives and children of his victims before their very eyes as they hung in agony? As a result of all this disorder, Palestine was invaded from all sides, even by Arab armies from the deserts to the south.

In the year 63 B.C., the Roman general Pompey arrived in Jerusalem with his legions. He had just cleared the Mediterranean of the pirates who swarmed in it, had conquered the last kings of Asia Minor, and had made Syria into a Roman province. Now, a fresh civil war gave him an excuse to intervene in Palestine. After a long siege, he captured the Holy City and made his entry into the Temple. He had heard that some great mystery was concealed in the sanctuary; so, curious and suspicious, his naked sword in his hand, he lifted the curtain of the Holy of Holies and entered. He emerged a disappointed man for, as we know, there was nothing to be seen inside!

From now on, the Romans were the masters of Israel. After Pompey came Caesar, the conqueror of Gaul and of Britain, who passed through Jerusalem on his way to Egypt. Then, after the murder of Caesar came Anthony and Octavius. It was they who, not wishing to make of Palestine a Roman province, gave it as a kingdom to the man who was destined to be the last King of Israel —Herod.

Here was shame, degradation, and misery for Israel! Herod was not even a Jew, but a half-breed Arab. He claimed to believe in the Lord, but if he did, his was a peculiar faith. The Commandments of God weighed little with him; a liar, a thief and a murderer, he seemed to have every possible vice. His best-loved wife, two of his sons, and many other people were put to death at his command. As he himself lay dying he summoned up the strength to order the execution of another of his sons whose rivalry he feared. This is the ferocious Herod whose name you read in the Life of Our Lord, for when he heard of the expected birth of Jesus, he ordered the slaughter of all the new-born children in the city so that this possible future rival should surely die.

It was in vain that Herod beautified Jerusalem with magnificent buildings and reconstructed the Temple on a larger and more sumptuous scale than even in the time of Solomon. It was in vain that he surrounded the enclosure with a gigantic colonnade, embellished the sanctuary with a vine of solid gold, and remade the seven-branched candlestick and the sacred fittings in precious materials. During the thirty-six years of his reign, all men trembled before him and none could be found to love him.

Thus the moment when its long history was coming to its close, we find God's chosen people once again in servitude and decadence. It is a sad ending, and one is inclined to ask, "How did God permit this to happen?" The answer is that the ways of God are not known to us, and that much happens in the world that is beyond the understanding of the human mind. We may, however, draw certain conclusions.

Did you ever notice how the life of a man draws to its close? Very often old age is accompanied by sickness and weakness; the limbs become enfeebled, sight and hearing fail. But, around the bedside of the old man we see a group of young people, full of strength and courage: his grandchildren. It is they who will take up the task abandoned by the worn hands of their grandfather, so that the torch is handed on from generation to generation.

Israel was now a very old nation; it had told the world all it had to say. And this was more than any other nation in the world has ever said. Its mission was ended, and another was about to begin. Christian teaching was now to succeed Jewish teaching, and in so doing to complete it and give it its full meaning.

It should be noted that the Jewish people themselves had some astonishing premonition in this mysterious matter. Some of them in their innermost hearts had already foreseen what was about to happen. They cherished within them one shining hope, the hope that, with the coming change, the Final Truth would be revealed to them.

XX

The Hope of Israel: The Coming of the Messias

WHAT WAS THIS HOPE that sustained the heart of Israel while the heavy tramp of the Roman legions resounded in her streets and while her people groaned under the savage rule of the usurper Herod? Listen carefully while I tell you, for it was the most shining hope that ever entered the heart of man.

"He will come!" the faithful Jews assured each other. "He will come and save us." "How peaceful and happy will be his reign," said one. "There will be justice for all," said another, while a third joined in, "Yes, when our Master comes all will be well, wonderfully well. Life will be grander even than in the reign of Solomon and more peaceful than in Abraham's day." So, as they chatted together beneath the porch of the Temple, the people consoled themselves for the miseries of the present.

Who, then, was this mysterious King, this beloved Master whose coming was so anxiously awaited? The people even had a name for him: the Messias, which roughly means, "the anointed of God," or, "the one chosen by God." As you see, the term was rather obscure and vague, but the people had to be satisfied with it. After all, it was rather a wonderful thing to know he was coming, this dispenser of justice, this all-powerful saviour.

How did they feel so certain about it? You remember of course the Prophets of Israel and the strange gift possessed by these inspired witnesses of God of seeing into the future. It was from these very prophecies that the people knew of the coming of the Messias;

it was because of the Prophets' teachings that they were prepared to listen to him. For centuries upon centuries throughout the long history of the chosen people, men inspired by God had foretold this coming. They had seen, far in future centuries, this splendid vision: there would one day be born a Man greater than all others, as rich in holiness as in power, who would complete the mission of Israel and reveal in full the truths about God. His coming would bring relief to all the misfortunes and miseries of mankind.

As far back as his day, Jacob on his deathbed, with his dear son Joseph standing by his side, had seen this consoling vision. King David had celebrated it with magnificent poetry in many of his Psalms. And again and again the great Prophets, Isaias, Ezechiel, and Daniel had asserted that the coming of the Messias was sure and certain, that one day Israel would be dazzled by his appearance in an immensity of joy.

We can well understand how the Jews cherished this promise in their hearts as misfortune overwhelmed them. It became for them a rock of comfort and consolation. Indeed they were unhappy, for Babylonians, Persians, Greeks, and Romans had polluted the Holy Land with their presence. But patience! The hour would come when all these sorrows would end, and when Israel's faith would be rewarded at last. The Messias would be born, the Saviour would come!

We must note, however, that the glimpses into the future which God permitted to the Prophets were not always clear in detail. The things foreseen were such a long way off and clouded in mystery. All men knew that the Messias was coming, but there were many questions to be answered about the exact conditions under which He would appear.

First of all, just who would this envoy of God be? In one of the most beautiful of all the Psalms we read that he would be "the Son of God." People often quoted the verse, "The Lord has said to me: Thou art My Son, this day have I begotten Thee. Ask of Me, and I will give thee . . . the utmost parts of the earth for thy possession."

At the same time, however, several of the Prophets stated that the Messias would be human, and some of them expressly called him the "Son of Man." This made things very hard to understand, for how could the "Son of God" be the "Son of Man" at the same time? Even the wisest and most learned of the scribes shook their heads when they tried to solve this seeming contradiction. They repeated these words of the Prophet Daniel, "I beheld in the vision of the night, and lo, one like the Son of Man came with the clouds of heaven, and he came even to the Ancient of days, and they presented him before Him. And He gave him power and glory, and a kingdom: and all peoples, tribes, and tongues shall serve him . . . and his kingdom shall not be destroyed." So, according to the prophecies, the Messias would be at the same time Son of Man and Son of God, mortal as we are, and immortal as God. No wonder the scribes shook their heads in puzzled bewilderment and searched the Bible texts more earnestly than ever for the smallest clue to the mystery.

They discovered in the writings of Isaias and Jeremias that the Messias would be a descendant of King David, but this was not a great deal of help, for in the course of a thousand years David's descendants had become very numerous and were to be found in every corner of Palestine. Another prophet, Micheas, had declared that he would be born in Bethlehem and this appeared equally strange, for Bethlehem was an obscure hamlet in Judea without distinction of any kind.

Finally, there was also a little phrase more puzzling than all the others. It was pronounced by the Prophet Isaias and was to the effect that the Messias would be "born of a virgin."

At the time of Herod's reign in Palestine, the coming of the Messias was a more burning subject of discussion and his appearance was awaited more eagerly than ever before. The reason for this impatience was another prophecy by the great Daniel, the same who had translated the writing on the wall for Baltasar. Daniel had declared that the Messias would come in "seventy weeks of years."

Now this amounted to four hundred and ninety years, and as the words had been uttered about five hundred years previously, people calculated that the time was over and that the coming of the Messias was at hand. No wonder they were impatient and filled with joyous anticipation!

Looking back from our day through all the centuries that have passed, we can see how perfectly all these events were arranged and how admirable was the Divine Plan. The further you progress in life, the more clearly you will realize how completely man's life is controlled by God. We all of us strive for our own personal interests and make plans for our future, but there is One much stronger than we are Who knows where all this is leading us, and all our efforts form part of His plan for us.

Think back on all you have learned of the history of Israel. So many trials and sufferings, so much courage and striving! In all their two thousand years of history, the gallant little nation knew scarcely one century free of warfare and suffering. And why? In order to maintain alive before mankind the idea that they alone possessed: the idea of the One True God. For what purpose was it that Moses received the Tablets of the Law on Mount Sinai; that David composed his superb poems; and that, often at the risk of their lives, the Prophets cried aloud the messages they had to give? Simply to prepare the world for the final revelation of truth, the revelation that would be brought by the Messias, Son of Man and Son of God.

It was not only the Israelites whom God used as His instruments in this preparation. Even the pagans had their own part to play in the Divine Plan. All the great empires whose rise and fall we have seen, did not come into being by chance. On the contrary, the kings and emperors who thought that their conquests were being made for their own glory were in fact only carrying out part of the plan ordained by God. Take Rome, for example. In three centuries the Roman empire had united all the countries of the Mediterranean basin and had even extended its boundaries to the Euphrates. Everywhere in the empire they made magnificent roads, so that travel was quick and easy, and Latin was the official language everywhere. In the end who profited most from the immense effort that went in to the building of the empire? It was the apostles of our Lord Jesus Christ who, a hundred years later, were to travel it from end to end, planting the Cross wherever they went.

God knows what He does, and He acts in His own good time. When the Messias would come, it would be to a world where everything was prepared to receive Him, a world where the holy men of Israel and the soldiers of Rome had labored to prepare the way for Him. Throughout the pagan world the minds of men were uneasy, for the most intelligent and learned among them knew well that their idols of stone and plaster counted for little, that there was no truth behind the not very edifying legends of the Greek gods and goddesses. Something more, they felt, was needed—but what it was they did not know. Not Israel alone, but the entire world, awaited the coming of its Saviour.

And yet, we all know what was to happen when Jesus did appear on earth, He who was truly the long-awaited Messias, the Saviour of the world. When He declared Himself to be the Christ—the Greek word for Messias—a great number of Jews refused to accept Him. His most extreme opponents, led by their priests, were to hatch a plot against Him, and after a mock trial were to submit Him to the most horrible and degrading torture, putting Him to death on the cross as though He were a slave.

What explanation can be found for this unspeakable tragedy? To know the reason for the appalling mistake made by Israel we must once again turn to the Bible. As I told you, and as you have seen for yourself, the Prophets gave few details about the manner in which the Messias would appear. Opinions differed greatly about the way in which He would reveal His power and proclaim His message. Reading the Scriptures carefully, two very different possibilities appeared to exist.

According to most of the prophecies, the Messias would come as a mighty and terrible king whose power no enemy could withstand. Richer than Solomon and braver than David, He would place Himself at the head of the army of Israel, and under His leadership all the enemies of Israel would be crushed. God's chosen people would become the mightiest nation on earth and would impose its will on all others.

Other students of the Bible could reply that this picture was

very far from the truth. "Study the Scriptures more closely," they would say, and they could point to other passages, much less numerous, which suggested an altogether different Messias. These spoke of a King of glory, who above all would be gentle, compassionate, a man of peace. In the writings of Isaias there were even some very touching verses which showed the Messias as a man like the rest of us, a man who would know deep suffering. And it was precisely these sufferings which He would offer to God as the price of our sins. The powers from which He would save us would not be those of hostile armies, but the powers of evil, the powers of sin—a salvation of a very different kind.

As we now know, this second interpretation was to come much closer to reality than the first one, but still it was not completely clear. Who could possibly have dreamed before it happened that the Son of God Himself, who could have been Lord of all the kingdoms of the earth, would consent to the most horrible suffering and death in order to wipe out the sins of us all? It was too great and too difficult a mystery for human understanding alone.

The real tragedy—and it is easy to understand—lay in the fact that the unhappy Jewish people, who had suffered so much at the hands of their enemies for the past six hundred years, very much preferred the first picture to the second. There was not much comfort to be found, they said, in the idea of a Messias who would submit to misery, persecution, and suffering. A much better idea was that of the King of glory, the mighty warrior who would lay low the enemies of Israel and restore the chosen people to their ancient splendor. There is the real reason why most of the Jews refused to accept Jesus.

Have *we* any right to condemn them for doing so? No, for they were only human beings like ourselves and, if we found ourselves in their place, how many of us would not have done as they did? How many of us, if we had to choose between suffering and glory, would not choose the second? Instead of hating the people who crucified Jesus, we should be grateful to them for all that they have given us of goodness and of truth. We should also remember those other Jews who were the friends and faithful followers of Christ: the Blessed Virgin, loveliest and gentlest of Jewish maidens, holy St. Joseph, the apostles who were the constant companions of the Messias during His life on earth, and St. Paul, who so staunchly preached His Word after His death. As for the others, can we do better than repeat Jesus' own words, "Father, forgive them, for they know not what they do."

Apart from all this, was not the fearful drama of the Crucifixion willed by God Himself, Who knows all things and Who can do all things? Was not the final revolt of Israel part of His Divine Plan? For when we come to sum up, we see that the great lesson that the world had still to learn, the lesson that would be taught by Christ Himself, was this: the worst slavery that man can endure is not that which is inflicted on him by human enemies but by his own sins, and that true liberty, like all the great things of life, can only be won through suffering and death.

And now, the story of God's chosen people is drawing to its close. Those of you who have followed it with me will not soon forget its splendors or the examples of heroic loyalty that shine through its pages. To cherish a lofty ideal and to sacrifice everything, even life itself, in order to preserve it—this is the noblest task that can fall to the lot of any man or of any people. Israel can point with just pride to the fact that, alone among the nations of the ancient world, her people, from generation to generation, remained true to the highest idea of all, the idea of the One True God.

There is a sequel to this story, an even more splendid one. It is the story of the real Messias, Our Lord Jesus Christ, who taught truth and love to the world. Perhaps one day, if you wish me to do so, and if it pleases God to permit it, I will tell it again for you.

NOTE . . . Counting Dates Before the Christian Era

I hope that you know what is meant by a date "before Jesus Christ," and that when I write "2000 years before our era," or "2000 years B.C.," you know what I mean. To be on the safe side, however, I think I had better explain.

Time passes continuously, so that the only way man can fix a point in time is by a system of dates. When you note in your diary that you have to go to a party on January 15, 1956, you are writing down a date, and dates are arrived at only by fairly difficult calculations.

In order to place themselves in time, men first of all selected the periods they could observe. The turning of the earth on its axis gave them the day; and its journey around the sun gave them the year. Next, the years were grouped into hundreds, and each period of one hundred years was called a century.

Now the problem was that, in order to put the centuries in numerical order, a starting-point must be fixed. Different nations chose as their starting-point some event of great importance in their history. For example, the Romans reckoned time from the day their city was founded (753 years before the birth of Christ). The Arabs fixed their starting-point by an event in the life of their prophet Mahomet which took place 622 years after the birth of Christ. For Christians, the date chosen was that which is to us the most important even in all the history of the world: the birth of Jesus Christ Himself in Bethlehem. By this we mean that when we write the date 1956 we are in the one thousand nine hundred and fifty-sixth year after the first of January of the first year following the birth of Christ. This method of counting dates is called the Christian era.

In order, however, to calculate dates before the birth of Christ, we simply reverse our method of counting. If you ever attended a race you will have noticed that the starter counts the seconds in diminishing figures: 10, 9, 8, 7, 6, and gave the signal to GO when he reached zero. After the start, the time-keeper measures the time of the race itself in ascending figures: 1, 2, 3, 4, 5, 6 . . . and so on. The dates of events that took place before the Christian era are measured in exactly the same way and the starting-point is the birth of Jesus.

You see, therefore, that before the Christian era, the higher the date, the older it is; 2000 B.C. is much further back than 1000 B.C. (The letters B.C. of course, stand for the words, "Before Christ.")

Before the time of Christ, therefore, the date of a man's birth is always higher than the date of his death, and the date of the commencement of a king's reign higher than the date of its end; for example, David was king from 1012 B.C. to 975 B.C. The twentieth century B.C. was further back in time than the nineteenth, the nineteenth further back than the eighteenth, and so on. In short, dates before Christ are reckoned in exactly the opposite manner to those which followed His birth. It is all very simple, and with a little practice you will soon get used to it.

An
ARKIVE EDITION
FROM SOPHIA INSTITUTE PRESS®

ARKive Editions are exact photographic reproductions of books published in previous decades or centuries. In them, you find undiluted by modern notions or passing fads the words and ideas of good and thoughtful souls who preceded us in this life.

In this, there is great value: it helps free us from the myopia that afflicts souls drowning in the words and images flooding forth from our modern media, with its attention focused so intently on that which is new and popular today.

Our age is less than perfect and ARKive Editions help us see that, enabling us to measure our own day by the often better standards of other times and places.

At the same time, previous ages and other cultures had their faults: and even in good books from earlier times we often find language, ideas, or values that were once deemed acceptable even by honorable souls, but are now seen clearly to be wrong.

We exclude from ARKive Editions books that have in them as significant themes ideas that are wrong. When, however, books that are overwhelmingly good are tainted by unfortunate peripheral remarks or occasional wrongheaded judgments, we have chosen to publish them intact. For we judge that the good to be done by such books far outweighs the harm done by occasional remarks which good men and women these days can (and should) dismiss as the unfortunate products of an age as flawed as our own, albeit in different ways.

If you disagree with our judgment, please understand, nonetheless, that we have sought to act in goodwill. Let your disagreement be an occasion for you to pray that our generation will soon come to see our own errors as clearly as we see the errors of earlier times; and then turn your attention back to the true riches that are to be found in each of our ARKive Editions, presented here exactly as they appeared to readers in earlier times.

For your free catalog, contact us at:

Sophia Institute Press®
Box 5284, Manchester, NH 03108
1-800-888-9344

www.SophiaInstitute.com

Sophia Institute® is a tax-exempt institution as defined by the Internal Revenue Code, Section 501(c)(3). Tax I.D. 22-2548708.